Inflammation is usually associated with swelling, redness and pain, but it's also a response to infection. It is linked to poor eating habits and obesity. If e____ inflammatory foods help bring a balance to inflammation in your body.

KT-145-659

"Antioxidants" seems to be a buzz word these days, but what's the real benefit? First, antioxidants fight off the over-production of free radicals. Second, these super-nutrients promote good health by fighting infections and diseases. And, in addition, they provide energy and even support skin health!

Some days you feel like you're ready to take on the world… other days you feel like you're in a fog, un-motivated, and you find it hard to focus. When you're having one of "those" days, enjoy brain-boosting foods to help you feel more alert and focused.

A bit of relaxation can go a long way and these foods help your body to naturally relax. These foods might not help you meet a deadline or pay off your mortgage any faster, but they will help you feel more calm and cool. Eat your way to a less stressful life!

We all want truly fabulous skin, but who wants to pay hundreds of dollars for the latest skin cream, hair treatment, or spa day? Certain foods can help your skin look more radiant, your hair shinier, and do we dare say… help you look younger?!

These foods will help your body naturally filter, cleanse, and essence nutrients efficiently. Certain foods have natural cleansing properties that help rid your body of the extra junk you put in and can help naturally curb your appetite!

Many digestive-related problems are directly associated with what you eat. These foods can help naturally balance your digestive system, provide digestive-related aid, and are high in nutritional value.

Have you ever been so tired at work that you fall asleep at your desk? Or even worse, nod off in a meeting? Keep these foods stashed at your desk to help fill you up, provide natural energy, and stay alert.

SUPER FOODS
ANTI-INFLAMMATORY

VEGETABLES	FRUITS	NUTS & SEEDS	HERBS & SPICES	OTHER
Tomatoes	Apples	Almonds	Basil	Cod
Avocados	Blueberries	Flaxseed/Linseed	Cayenne/Chili Peppers	Halibut
Peppers	Fresh Pineapple	Hazelnuts	Cinnamon/Cloves	Oysters
Bok Choy	Guavas	Sunflower Seeds	Cocoa (70%+ cocoa)	Salmon
Broccoli	Kiwi	Walnuts	Licorice	Shrimp
Brussels Sprouts	Lemons/ Limes		Mint	Tuna
Cabbage	Oranges		Oregano	Turkey
Cauliflower	Papaya		Parsley	Lamb
Chard	Raspberries		Rosemary	
Fennel	Strawberries		Thyme	
Bulb Garlic			Turmeric	
Green Beans				
Green/Spring Onions				
Kale				
Leeks				
Olives				
Spinach				
Sweet Potatoes				
Turnip Greens				

PULSE IT UP!

YOUR GUIDE TO UNLOCK THE POWER OF FOOD

150+ DELICIOUS RECIPES

Pascoe Publishing, Inc.
Rocklin, California

© 2011, Euro-Pro, LLC.

All rights reserved. No portion of this book may be reproduced by any means whatsoever without written permission from EuroPro, LLC., except for the inclusion of quotations in a media review.

Although every precaution has been taken in the preparation of this book, the publisher and authors assume no responsibility for errors or omissions. Nor is any liability assumed for damages resulting from the use of the information contained herein. Although every effort has been made to ensure that the information contained in this book is complete and accurate, neither the publisher nor the authors are engaged in rendering professional advice or services to the individual reader. This information is not intended to replace the advice of a medical practitioner and consumers should always consult with a health care professional prior to making changes to diet or lifestyle, including any new health-related eating programs. Neither the publisher nor author shall be held responsible for any loss or damage allegedly arising from any information or suggestion in this book. The opinions expressed in this book represent the personal views of the authors and not that of the publisher.

Nutritional Analyses: Calculations for the nutritional analyses in this book are based on the largest number of servings listed within the recipes. Calculations are rounded up to the nearest gram or milligram, as appropriate. If two options for an ingredient are listed, the first one is used. Not included are optional ingredients or serving suggestions.

Cover & Interior Design: KB Designs | Photography: Austin Blanco | Food Stylist: Michael Gadwa | Editor: Debi Bock

Published in the United States of America by

Pascoe Publishing, Inc.
Rocklin, California
www. pascoepublishing. com

ISBN: 978-1-929862-88-7

10   9   8   7   6   5   4   3   2   .

Printed in China

TABLE OF CONTENTS

INTRODUCTION

Inside these pages, we've compiled the latest nutritional information to teach you how to combine ingredients to get the maximum healthful benefits from delicious and flavorful recipes. We aren't preaching to you to become a crazy health nut; we are simply offering a practical way to improve the things you blend, enabling a healthy lifestyle.

Although our goal in *Pulse it Up!* was to develop "healthy" recipes, our most important requirement was for each recipe to taste great! We know you don't have time to study this chapter, so we've made it easy for you to quickly identify the primary benefits of each recipe with our "Health Highlights". Each recipe outlines the main benefits on the side tabs of the page, allowing you to quickly choose recipes with the benefits you need. Whether you woke up feeling groggy and need a boost of energy to your morning, or you're looking for a dose of relaxation after a long day, you can quickly find delicious recipes tailored just for you!

The next few pages are your guide to understanding the Health Highlights and the Food Glossary that follows showcases some of nature's very best foods. So, go on…plug in your Ninja™ Kitchen System Pulse and blend delicious smoothies, knead dough into mouth-watering flatbreads and pastries, juice whole fruits and vegetables, and chop fresh ingredients for tasty snacks.

Above all… unlock the power of food and let our complete system inspire and simplify healthy living for your active on-the-go lifestyle.

Here's to your good health!

The Ninja™ Team

HEALTH HIGHLIGHTS

ANTI-INFLAMMATORY

IMMUNE BOOST

MENTAL BOOST

RELAXATION & STRESS RELIEF

ANTI-AGING: SKIN, HAIR & EYE HEALTH

DETOXIFY & MANAGE WEIGHT

DIGESTION

ENERGY BOOST

SUPER FOODS
IMMUNE BOOST

VEGETABLES	FRUITS	NUTS & SEEDS	HERBS & SPICES	OTHER
Garlic	Blueberries	Pecans	Turmeric	Yogurt
Mushrooms	Lemons	Almonds	Black Pepper	Pinto Beans
Sweet Potatoes	Grapefruit	Flaxseed	Oregano	Kidney Beans
Carrots	Tangerines		Cinnamon	Black Beans
Cucumbers	Oranges		Cloves	
Pumpkin	Grapes		Ginger	
Squash	Raisins		Cayenne Pepper	
Cabbage	Plums		Sage	
Spinach	Strawberries		Thyme	
Kale	Raspberries		Basil	
Peppers	Cherries			
Brussels Sprouts	Watermelon			
Broccoli	Nectarines			
Artichokes	Peaches			
Russet Potatoes	Mangos			
Green Beans	Melon			
Tomato	Apricots			
	Blackberries			
	Apples			
	Cranberries			
	Pineapple			
	Kiwi			

SUPER FOODS
MENTAL BOOST

VEGETABLES	FRUITS	NUTS & SEEDS	HERBS & SPICES	OTHER
Beets	Blueberries	Walnuts	Turmeric	Salmon
Broccoli	Lemons/Limes	Cashews	Rosemary	Eggs
Carrots	Oranges	Peanuts		Coffee, Freshly Ground
Romaine Lettuce	Grapefruit	Flaxseed		Beans
Spinach	Apricots			Kidney Beans
Swiss Chard	Mangos			Pinto Beans
Rocket	Cantaloupe			Shrimp
Kale	Watermelon			
Tomatoes	Strawberries			
Radishes	Blackberries			
Aubergine	Raspberries			
	Cranberries			
	Cherries			
	Plums			

SUPER FOODS
RELAXATION & STRESS RELIEF

VEGETABLES	FRUITS	NUTS & SEEDS	HERBS & SPICES	OTHER
Broccoli	Blueberries	Walnuts	Basil	Low fat/Skim Milk
Kale	Oranges	Almonds		Brown Rice
Brussels Sprouts	Bananas	Pistachios		Salmon
Asparagus	Apples	Pumpkin Seeds		Shrimp
Cabbage	Pomegranates	Sunflower Seeds		Scallops
Artichokes	Pineapple			Tuna
Sweet Potatoes	Apricots			
Avocados	Papayas			
Black Beans				
Corn				
White Beans				
Potatoes				
Lentils				
Chickpeas				
Spinach				
Swiss Chard				
Asparagus				
Rocket				

SUPER FOODS
ANTI-AGING: SKIN, HAIR & EYE HEALTH

VEGETABLES	FRUITS	NUTS & SEEDS	HERBS & SPICES	OTHER
Avocado	Watermelon	Pumpkin Seeds	Ginger	Herring
Garlic	Blackberries	Sunflower Seeds	Cinnamon	Salmon
Broccoli	Blueberries	Walnuts	Sage	Shrimp
Cherry Tomatoes	Strawberries	Brazil Nuts		Fresh Tuna
Spinach	Red Grapes	Almonds		Dark Chocolate
Red Onions	Cranberries			Kidney Beans
Cauliflower	Raspberries			Pinto Beans
Cucumbers	Oranges			Yogurt
Kale	Cherries			Cottage Cheese
Turnips	Plums			
Brussels Sprouts	Mangos			
Cabbage	Grapefruit			
Radish	Peaches			
Artichoke Hearts	Cantaloupe			
Carrots	Pineapple			
Squash	Kiwi			
Bok Choy	Honeydew			
Peas				

SUPER FOODS
DETOXIFY & MANAGE WEIGHT

VEGETABLES	FRUITS	NUTS & SEEDS	HERBS & SPICES	OTHER
Artichoke	Blackberries	Flaxseed	Cayenne Pepper	Salmon
Broccoli	Blueberries	Sunflower Seeds	Ginger	Eggs
Cauliflower	Cherries	Pine Nuts	Cinnamon	Shrimp
Green Beans	Purple Grapes		Horseradish	Lean Meats
Sweet Potatoes	Kiwi		Red Chili Peppers	Yogurt
Yams	Papayas			Milk
Beans	Prunes			Cheese
Spinach	Raspberries			
Asparagus	Strawberries			
Tomatoes	Grapefruit			
Mushrooms	Apples			
Cucumbers	Watermelon			
Peppers	Cantaloupe			
Celery				
Carrots				

SUPER FOODS
DIGESTION

VEGETABLES	FRUITS	NUTS & SEEDS	HERBS & SPICES	OTHER
Garlic	Apples	Sunflower Seeds	Mint	Yogurt
Avocados	Bananas	Flaxseed Oil	Cumin	Rice
Cabbage	Blackberries	Almonds	Fennel	Tofu
Onion	Blueberries		Oregano	Eggs
Squash	Cherries		Curry Powder	
Cucumbers	Purple Grapes		Paprika	
Broccoli	Papaya		Basil	
Romaine Lettuce	Lemons		Sage	
Kale	Raisins		Cumin	
Onions	Mangos		Mustard	
Beans			Garlic	
			Cinnamon	
			Paprika	
			Coriander	
			Cayenne Pepper	
			Ginger	
			Clove	
			Coriander	

SUPER FOODS
ENERGY BOOST

VEGETABLES	FRUITS	NUTS & SEEDS	HERBS & SPICES	OTHER
Beans	Oranges	Almonds	Parsley	Yogurt
Spinach	Watermelon	Pumpkin Seeds	Coriander	Eggs
Romaine Lettuce	Blackberries	Hazelnuts		Salmon
Corn	Blueberries	Cashews		Lean Meats
Sweet Potatoes	Raspberries	Flaxseeds		Tuna
Spinach	Apples			Shrimp
Celery	Strawberries			Whole Grain Pasta
Cucumbers	Kiwi			Dark Chocolate
Mushrooms	Cantaloupe			Steak
Lentils	Bananas			
Avocados	Grapefruit			
Watercress	Pears			
Rocket	Lemons			
Kale				
Beans				

APPLES

THE ADVANTAGE:

- Really strong antioxidant power!
- A true healing-power food
- The second-highest level of antioxidant activity of any consumed fruit
- Valuable source of fibre, which can lower cholesterol
- Contains the highest source of Boron, a mineral that assists in bone-building.

FOOD FOR THOUGHT:

- The apple peel has the most potent antioxidant activity.
- Purchased apple juice may have added sugar and preservatives, along with higher calories. Make your own at home as the best alternative.

BANANAS

THE ADVANTAGE:

- Bananas are a rich source of Vitamin B6, which may prolong mental health, according to the USDA.
- High in potassium and fibre

FOOD FOR THOUGHT:

- Bananas are rich in potassium, which can help maintain body fluids, assist heart health, balance electrolytes, reduce muscle cramps, and elevate energy levels.
- Assists in good digestive health.
- The inner peel is one of the most nutritional parts! Scrape the inner peel into your smoothie for an added nutritional boost!

BLUEBERRIES

THE ADVANTAGE:

- This little fruit packs a big punch that helps keep your memory sharp and your brain stimulated.
- One of the most powerful fruits to include in your diet
- Blueberries provide strong antioxidant power, act as an anti-inflammatory, and may help with your memory.

FOOD FOR THOUGHT:

- Either fresh or frozen berries deliver the same delicious, healthy benefits.
- Blue and Purple fruit are memory-boosters.

CANTALOUPE

The Advantage:

- Cantaloupe is your best friend in weight control. Why? It is a high-volume fruit that curbs hunger: high in fibre, water and air, yet low in calories. Your body thinks you're full faster, with less craving for more.
- Rich in potassium and Vitamin A, which helps heart-health, blood pressure, vision, growth and bone-building.
- High in Vitamin C!
- One of the best immune boosters among all fruits!

FOOD FOR THOUGHT:

- Cantaloupe is rich in Vitamin A as a beta carotene. It helps protect against cell damage and is a great antioxidant.

TASTE THE ADVANTAGE:

- Mix cantaloupe with watermelon, club soda, and fresh ginger for a refreshing treat.

RASPBERRIES

THE ADVANTAGE:

- A fibre powerhouse!
- The benefits don't stop there; raspberries have magnesium and, not to mention, are low in calories.
- Help replace dying cells with healthy cells, may help with inflammation and pain.
- Significant antioxidant boost.

FOOD FOR THOUGHT:

- This fruit is fragile: we recommend buying fresh and organic for best nutritional value and flavor satisfaction.
- Highest count of fibre among the most commonly eaten berries.

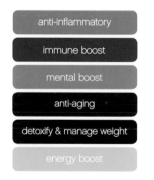

STRAWBERRIES

THE ADVANTAGE:

- Potent antioxidant berry.
- Offers the most Vitamin C of any other commonly consumed berry.
- Red fruits can help improve blood flow and are thought to help prevent Alzheimer's disease.

FOOD FOR THOUGHT:

- 150g of strawberries equals about 50 calories and offers around 3g of fibre and around 85mg of Vitamin C.
- Noted as one of the most contaminated fruits. Buy organic to get the best flavor and quality.
- Frozen strawberries offer the same health benefits as fresh, a great alternative year round.
- High in disease-fighting phytochemicals.

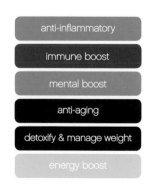

PINEAPPLE	ORANGES	KIWI

THE ADVANTAGE:

- Powerful anti-inflammatory powers.
- Contains Bromelain enzymes, natural blood thinners, that can aid in digestion, healing and inflammation.
- Provides fibre, Vitamin C, potassium, and other minerals for general good health.
- Yellow and Orange fruits help prevent eye disease and act as an immune boost.

FOOD FOR THOUGHT:

- One of the most powerful natural digestive reliefs.
- 165g of fresh pineapple has almost 100% of the daily value for manganese. Manganese is essential for healthy skin, cartilage formation and bones.

THE ADVANTAGE:

- A massive boost of Vitamin C, a premier antioxidant.
- Provides support for better heart and digestive health and lowers the risk of infections, inflammation and stroke.
- May also improve healthful cholesterol.
- Contains high amounts of calcium, which promotes strong bones and teeth.

FOOD FOR THOUGHT:

- Studies have shown citrus fruits may lower the risk of some cancers.
- Pulp is your friend! Pulp contains the healthiest nutrients in fruits, providing many vitamin compounds, minerals and fibre.

THE ADVANTAGE:

- A super-fruit, rich with antioxidants, that can help in healing.
- Kiwis have the highest level of Vitamin C, twice that of oranges.
- A good source of Vitamin E, potassium, and fibre.

FOOD FOR THOUGHT:

- Kiwi works as a natural blood thinner.
- Green fruits can help protect bones and teeth, and aid in eyesight.
- A natural meat tenderizer, cut kiwi in half and rub on meat before cooking.

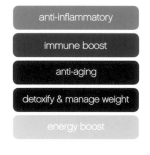

WATERMELON

THE ADVANTAGE:

- One of the healthiest foods! Watermelon helps curb your appetite and provides high levels of lycopene and Vitamin A.
- A high-volume food which aids in managing weight.
- Great source of vitamin A as a beta-carotene that helps fight free radicals, essential for eye and immune health.

FOOD FOR THOUGHT:

- Helps support eye and immune health via Vitamin A (in beta-carotene), which helps fight free radicals.
- Watermelon is great after a workout. It can help re-hydrate your body and restore electrolyte balance.

immune boost

mental boost

anti-aging

detoxify & manage weight

energy boost

AVOCADOS

THE ADVANTAGE:

- Although high in fat; the fact is, it's a healthy HDL fat. Monounsaturated fat is an omega-9 that may actually lower cholesterol.
- Contains lutein from the carotene family that acts as an antioxidant to aid in eye, heart and skin health.
- Avocados are a great source of fibre, potassium, folate, Vitamin A, Vitamin E, Zinc and beta-carotene.
- Rich in folate, in the Vitamin B family, that may help prevent birth defects.

FOOD FOR THOUGHT:

- Research studies link avocados to lower blood pressure and cholesterol counts. Helpful in maintaining bone and immune health.

anti-inflammatory

relaxation & stress relief

anti-aging

digestion

KALE

THE ADVANTAGE:

- Superstar vegetable! The #1 antioxidant food that fights cell-damaging free radicals.
- Contains phyto-chemicals that have been shown to have protective effects against many cancers.
- Loaded with calcium, Vitamin A, C, K, and iron.
- Terrific source of fibre and protein.

FOOD FOR THOUGHT:

- Kale has seven times the beta-carotene of broccoli.

anti-inflammatory

immune boost

mental boost

relaxation & stress relief

anti-aging

TOMATOES

THE ADVANTAGE:

- Provides extremely beneficial anti-cancer properties when consumed with fat-rich foods such as avocados. Fat-rich foods help the absorption of lycopene.
- Tomatoes contain multiple antioxidant agents that have strong disease fighting power.
- A mega dose of Vitamin C, rich in potassium and magnesium, this powerful combo is a great choice to restore your body after a workout.

FOOD FOR THOUGHT:

- May be especially good for men; the antioxidant compounds have been shown to fight prostate cancer.

immune boost

mental boost

anti-aging

detoxify & manage weight

SPINACH

THE ADVANTAGE:

- One of the best sources of Vitamin K, critical for building strong bones. Vitamin K works with calcium to make sure you get the minerals into your bones.
- It's also rich in Vitamin A, manganese, folic acid, magnesium, iron, and quercetin (anti-inflamatory compound).
- Promotes good health as an antioxidant and anti-cancer support.
- May help lower cholesterol and blood pressure while assisting eye and heart-health. Can also help reduce inflammation.

FOOD FOR THOUGHT:

- Spinach provides more nutrients than almost any other food.
- One of the lowest calorie foods on the planet.
- A great alternative to milk for Vitamin C.

BROCCOLI

THE ADVANTAGE:

- Strong antioxidant and aid in detoxifying.
- 70g of broccoli contains more than 40mg of calcium, 81 mg of Vitamin C, 2g of protein and fibre, a whopping 1,277 mcg of Vitamin A, plus folate, magnesium, phosphorus and beta-carotene.
- Great for bone, teeth, and eye health.

FOOD FOR THOUGHT:

- Broccoli has been shown to help fight cancers by neutralizing carcinogens that destroy cancerous cells.
- May be especially good for women; broccoli is linked to reducing the risk of breast and cervical cancer.

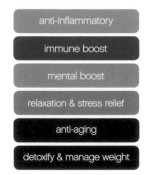

CARROTS

THE ADVANTAGE:

- Contains a high level of carotenoids, which are associated with decreasing the risk of cancer.
- A great source of lutein, which provides eye health.
- Antioxidant and immune system stimulator, helpful in fighting infections.
- Rich source of calcium, potassium, Vitamin A and sprinkled with magnesium, phosphorus and fibre.
- Fantastic for detoxifying!

FOOD FOR THOUGHT:

- Recent studies have indicated a carrot a day could cut the rate of lung cancer.
- Yellow and Orange fruits help with eye health and can boost your immune system.

CHAPTER TWO :: APPETIZERS, SNACKS & SALSAS

AVOCADO SHAKE – P. 88

anti-inflammatory

immune boost

mental boost

relaxation &
stress relief

detoxify &
manage weight

digestion

FIERY CHILE SHRIMP
WITH FRESH ROCKET

15ml TOASTED SESAME OIL

30ml RICE WINE VINEGAR (OR 1 TBSP. WHITE VINEGAR)

30ml WATER

½ SMALL FRESH CHILLI (OR TO TASTE), ROUGHLY CUT

½ SMALL TOMATO

½ SMALL WHITE ONION, ROUGHLY CUT

2 CLOVES GARLIC, PEELED

2g FRESH CORIANDER LEAVES

SALT & PEPPER TO TASTE

20 LARGE COOKED SHRIMP, DEVEINED AND TAILS REMOVED

15g FRESH ROCKET, WASHED AND DRAINED

Place all ingredients, except the shrimp and rocket, in the 1.1L Processing Bowl and pulse until lightly chopped. Remove and place in a medium bowl. To serve, arrange the shrimp on rocket leaves on 4 small plates and spoon the fiery tomato topping over each. Serve immediately or chill until serving. Serves 4.

CAL 75, FAT 0G, SAT FAT 0G, CHOL 47MG, SODIUM 53MG,
CARBS 4G, PROTEIN 2G, FIBRE 1G, CALCIUM 25MG, POTASSIUM 203MG

immune boost

mental boost

anti-aging: skin, hair & eye health

detoxify & manage weight

QUICK & EASY
GOLDEN TREASURE CARROTS

30ml ORANGE JUICE

250g LOW FAT CREAM CHEESE, AT ROOM TEMPERATURE

40g RAW, UNFILTERED HONEY

PINCH GROUND GINGER

PINCH GROUND CINNAMON

1 LB. FRESH CARROTS, PEELED, CUT INTO 5mm THICK COINS, BLANCHED AND CHILLED (OR SERVE FRESH, RAW CARROT COINS, IF DESIRED)

Place the orange juice, cream cheese, honey, and spices in the 1.1L Processing Bowl. Pulse until smooth. Spoon into a small bowl and serve with the chilled carrot coins. Serves 4 to 6.

**CAL 144, FAT 7G, SAT FAT 4G, CHOL 21MG, SODIUM 164MG,
CARBS 16G, PROTEIN 5G, FIBRE 2G, CALCIUM 69MG, POTASSIUM 326MG**

Vertical side tabs:
anti-inflammatory
immune boost
relaxation & stress relief
anti-aging: skin, hair & eye health
detoxify & manage weight
digestion
energy boost

BLACK BEAN DIP
WITH MELTED GOAT CHEESE

425g CAN BLACK BEANS, DRAINED, LIQUID RESERVED

1 CLOVE GARLIC, PEELED

1g FRESH CORIANDER LEAVES

10ml FRESH LIME JUICE

1g GROUND CUMIN

1g CHILI POWDER (OR MORE, TO TASTE)

1g SALT

115g GOAT CHEESE, CRUMBLED

FRESH VEGETABLES FOR DIPPING: BROCCOLI FLORETS,

RED PEPPER STRIPS, CELERY, CAULIFLOWER FLORETS, ETC.

Preheat oven to 190°C/Gas Mark 5. Place all ingredients, except the goat cheese, in the 1.1L Processing Bowl. Pulse until smooth.

Place the bean dip in an oven-proof serving dish and top with the goat cheese. Bake for 10-12 minutes, or until the goat cheese has melted. Serve with fresh vegetables for dipping. Serves 6 to 8.

CAL 116, FAT 3G, SAT FAT 2G, CHOL 2MG, SODIUM 31MG,

CARBS 14G, PROTEIN 5G, FIBRE 5G, CALCIUM 20MG, POTASSIUM 243MG

anti-inflammatory

mental boost

relaxation &
stress relief

ITALIAN BRUSCHETTA
WITH CREAMY BALSAMIC SPREAD

**1 BAGUETTE, SLICED INTO 1cm THICK
ROUNDS**

60ml EXTRA VIRGIN OLIVE OIL

170g CAN SLICED BLACK OLIVES, DIVIDED

400g CAN CHICKPEAS, DRAINED

15ml BALSAMIC VINEGAR

PINCH RED PEPPER FLAKES

1 CLOVE GARLIC, PEELED

6g SALT

PINCH GROUND BLACK PEPPER

**8g FLAT-LEAF PARSLEY, CHOPPED,
FOR GARNISH**

Preheat the broiler to High. Brush each baguette slice generously with olive oil on one side and place on the broiler pan, oiled side up. Broil until toasted and set aside.

Place one-half of the olives and the remaining ingredients, except the parsley, in the 1.1L Processing Bowl. Pulse until smooth. To serve, spoon a small amount of the balsamic spread on each toast and garnish with the remaining sliced olives and parsley. Serves 6 to 8.

**CAL 265, FAT 8G, SAT FAT 1G, CHOL 0MG, SODIUM 1064MG,
CARBS 44G, PROTEIN 8G, FIBRE 5G, CALCIUM 29MG, POTASSIUM 156MG**

anti-inflammatory

immune boost

mental boost

relaxation & stress relief

anti-aging: skin, hair & eye health

detoxify & manage weight

digestion

energy boost

FAST & FRESH SPINACH
& CHEDDAR CHEESE QUICHE

1 SHEET REFRIGERATED PIE DOUGH

6 LARGE EGGS

30ml LOW FAT MILK

30g FRESH SPINACH LEAVES, ROUGHLY CUT

85g CHEDDAR CHEESE, SHREDDED

2 SPRING ONIONS, ROUGHLY CUT

6g SALT

PINCH GROUND BLACK PEPPER

Unfold the pastry sheet into a large 36cm sauté pan and cut the pastry in a circle to fit the bottom of the pan only. Cook the pastry crust on medium-low heat for 5 to 6 minutes, or until firm on the bottom. Using a wide spatula, flip the pastry and continue cooking for 3 to 4 minutes.

Place the remaining ingredients in the 1.1L Processing Bowl and pulse until the spinach and onions are chopped. Pour the egg mixture over the pastry. Cover and cook over medium heat until the eggs are set and the quiche is cooked throughout, about 8 to 10 minutes. Slice into thin wedges and serve while warm. Serves 8.

CAL 200, FAT 13G, SAT FAT 6G, CHOL 152MG, SODIUM 543MG,
CARBS 13G, PROTEIN 8G, FIBRE 0G, CALCIUM 77MG, POTASSIUM 90MG

EDAMAME DIP
WITH BROCCOLI FLORETS

310g PACKAGE FROZEN SHELLED EDAMAME, BLANCHED

30ml SOY SAUCE (OR USE LOW SODIUM SOY SAUCE)

8g FRESH CORIANDER LEAVES

40g SWEET ONION, ROUGHLY CUT

1 CLOVE GARLIC, PEELED

30ml EXTRA VIRGIN OLIVE OIL

60g SOUR CREAM (USE LOW FAT, IF PREFERRED)

2 MEDIUM HEADS BROCCOLI, CUT INTO FLORETS

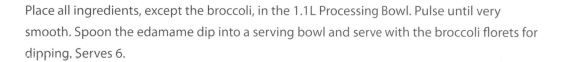

Place all ingredients, except the broccoli, in the 1.1L Processing Bowl. Pulse until very smooth. Spoon the edamame dip into a serving bowl and serve with the broccoli florets for dipping. Serves 6.

**CAL 237, FAT 14G, SAT FAT 4G, CHOL 9MG, SODIUM 345MG,
CARBS 15G, PROTEIN 14G, FIBRE 7G, CALCIUM 196MG, POTASSIUM 871MG**

anti-inflammatory

immune boost

mental boost

relaxation & stress relief

anti-aging: skin, hair & eye health

detoxify & manage weight

energy boost

anti-inflammatory

immune boost

mental boost

relaxation &
stress relief

anti-aging; skin,
hair & eye health

detoxify &
manage weight

digestion

energy boost

SMOKED SALMON SPREAD

250g LOW FAT CREAM CHEESE, AT ROOM TEMPERATURE.

60g LOW FAT SOUR CREAM

50g LOW FAT GREEK YOGURT

15ml FRESH LEMON JUICE

2g FRESH DILL, PLUS MORE FOR GARNISH

2g CHIVES (OR SPRING ONIONS), PLUS MORE FOR GARNISH

3g SALT

PINCH GROUND BLACK PEPPER

115g SMOKED SALMON, ROUGHLY CHOPPED

THINLY SLICED RYE BREAD ROUNDS

Place the cream cheese, sour cream, yogurt, lemon juice, dill, chives, salt, pepper, and half of the smoked salmon in the 1.1L Processing Bowl. Pulse until smooth.

Place the spread in a serving dish and mix in the remaining salmon by hand. Garnish with dill and chives, if desired. Serve right away with rye bread rounds or chill until serving. Serves 8.

CAL 95, FAT 6G, SAT FAT 4G, CHOL 20MG, SODIUM 347MG,
CARBS 3G, PROTEIN 7G, FIBRE 0G, CALCIUM 54MG, POTASSIUM 74MG

COURGETTE ROLLS STUFFED WITH HERBED GOAT CHEESE

230g FRESH GOAT CHEESE, AT ROOM TEMPERATURE

30ml LOW FAT MILK

2g FRESH MINT LEAVES

2g FRESH BASIL LEAVES

3g FRESH CHIVES

2g LEMON ZEST (OR JUICE, IF DESIRED)

3 LARGE COURGETTE, SLICED LENGTHWISE INTO 5mm SLICES AND BROILED OR GRILLED

Place all of the ingredients, except the courgette, in the 1.1L Processing Bowl. Pulse until smooth.

Put one-half teaspoon of the cheese mixture about 1cm from the end of each cooled courgette slice. Roll up each slice and place seam side down on a serving platter. Secure with toothpicks, if needed. Serve right away or chill until serving. Serves 4 to 6.

**CAL 166, FAT 9G, SAT FAT 6G, CHOL 23MG, SODIUM 160MG,
CARBS 5G, PROTEIN 2G, FIBRE 1G, CALCIUM 29MG, POTASSIUM 368MG**

immune boost

anti-aging: skin, hair & eye health

detoxify & manage weight

digestion

anti-inflammatory

immune boost

mental boost

relaxation &
stress relief

detoxify &
manage weight

TOMATO BASIL BRUSCHETTA

2 MEDIUM ROMA TOMATOES, SEEDED, CORED, AND QUARTERED

1 CLOVE GARLIC, PEELED

10 LARGE FRESH BASIL LEAVES

30ml EXTRA VIRGIN OLIVE OIL

10g CAPERS

1 BAGUETTE, SLICED INTO 5mm THICK ROUNDS, TOASTED

Place the tomatoes, garlic, basil and olive oil in the 1.1L Processing Bowl. Pulse just until roughly chopped. Mix in the capers by hand.

Place a tablespoon of the tomato mixture on each baguette round and arrange the bruschetta on a serving platter. Serve right away. Serves 4 to 6.

CAL 195, FAT 6G, SAT FAT 1G, CHOL 0MG, SODIUM 414MG,
CARBS 31G, PROTEIN 0G, FIBRE 1G, CALCIUM 9MG, POTASSIUM 54MG

PINEAPPLE & RED ONION SALSA

40g RED ONION, ROUGHLY CUT

3g FRESH CORIANDER LEAVES

330g FRESH PINEAPPLE, ROUGHLY CUT

20g RAW, UNFILTERED HONEY

30ml FRESH LIME JUICE

Place all the ingredients in the 1.1L Processing Bowl and pulse quickly, just until chunky.
Serve right away over mild white fish or poultry. Serves 6 to 8.

CAL 49, FAT 0G, SAT FAT 0G, CHOL 0MG, SODIUM 2MG,
CARBS 14G, PROTEIN 0G, FIBRE 1G, CALCIUM 1MG, POTASSIUM 115MG

anti-inflammatory

immune boost

relaxation &
stress relief

anti-aging: skin,
hair & eye health

digestion

energy boost

anti-inflammatory

immune boost

mental boost

relaxation &
stress relief

anti-aging, skin,
hair & eye health

detoxify &
manage weight

digestion

CHERRY TOMATO BITES

24 LARGE CHERRY TOMATOES

1 LARGE RIPE AVOCADO, SEEDED AND SKIN REMOVED

115g FETA CHEESE, CRUMBLED

15ml LEMON JUICE

9g CHIVES

SALT TO TASTE

Slice 5mm off the bottom of each tomato, reserving the slices. Remove the juice, seeds, and flesh from the inside of each cherry tomato. Set aside, stem side down.

Place the remaining ingredients in the 1.1L Processing Bowl. Pulse until smooth.

Place 1 teaspoon of the avocado mixture into each cherry tomato. Top each with a reserved tomato slice. Makes 24 appetizers.

CAL 124, FAT 9G, SAT FAT 4G, CHOL 17MG, SODIUM 239MG,
CARBS 8G, PROTEIN 3G, FIBRE 2G, CALCIUM 10MG, POTASSIUM 177MG

anti-inflammatory

immune boost

relaxation &
stress relief

digestion

energy boost

EAST INDIAN SPICED LENTIL DIP
WITH NAAN BREAD

15ml FRESH LEMON JUICE

15ml EXTRA VIRGIN OLIVE OIL

PINCH GROUND CUMIN

PINCH GROUND CORIANDER

1g SALT

PINCH GROUND BLACK PEPPER

290g RED LENTILS, COOKED

¼ SWEET ONION, ROUGHLY CUT

2 CLOVES GARLIC, PEELED

½ JALAPEÑO PEPPER, SEEDED, ROUGHLY CUT

1 OR 2 INDIAN NAAN BREADS, TORN INTO BITE-SIZED PIECES

Place the juice, oil, cumin, coriander, salt and pepper in the 1.1L Processing Bowl. Pulse 3 times. Add the lentils, onion, garlic and pepper. Pulse until smooth. Chill very well before serving with the bread. Serves 3 to 4.

**CAL 206, FAT 6G, SAT FAT 0G, CHOL 0MG, SODIUM 148MG,
CARBS 30G, PROTEIN 7G, FIBRE 6G, CALCIUM 20MG, POTASSIUM 343MG**

anti-inflammatory

immune boost

mental boost

detoxify &
manage weight

energy boost

FIRE-ROASTED TOMATO SALSA
WITH TORTILLA CHIPS

415g FIRE-ROASTED TOMATOES, WITH JUICE

½ SMALL RED ONION, PEELED, ROUGHLY CUT

4 CLOVES GARLIC, PEELED

3g SALT

PINCH GROUND BLACK PEPPER

PINCH GROUND CUMIN

4g FRESH CORIANDER LEAVES

30ml FRESH LIME JUICE

170g BAKED TORTILLA CHIPS

Place all ingredients, except the chips, in the 1.1L Processing Bowl and pulse until fairly smooth. Taste and adjust seasonings, as desired. Serve right away with tortilla chips or refrigerate for up to 2 days. Makes about 390g.

**CAL 110, FAT 1G, SAT FAT 0G, CHOL 0MG, SODIUM 305MG,
CARBS 22G, PROTEIN 2G, FIBRE 2G, CALCIUM 55MG, POTASSIUM 229MG**

anti-inflammatory

immune boost

detoxify &
manage weight

energy boost

TOMATILLO SALSA VERDE

450g GREEN TOMATILLOS, HUSKS, SEEDS AND PULP REMOVED

1 FRESH CHILLI, SEEDED, ROUGHLY CUT

80g WHITE ONION, ROUGHLY CUT

4g FRESH CORIANDER LEAVES

15ml FRESH LIME JUICE

1g SUGAR

3g SALT

4 WHOLE WHEAT TORTILLAS, TORN AND BROILED UNTIL CRISPY

Place the tomatillos in a medium saucepan and cover with water. Bring to a boil on high heat. When the water boils, reduce the heat and simmer for 5 minutes. Drain. Cool slightly and place in the 1.1L Processing Bowl. Add the remaining ingredients, except the tortillas, and pulse until almost smooth. Serve with the tortilla crisps. Makes 4 servings.

CAL 171, FAT 5G, SAT FAT 1G, CHOL 0MG, SODIUM 809MG,
CARBS 97G, PROTEIN 5G, FIBRE 3G, CALCIUM 51MG, POTASSIUM 147MG

anti-inflammatory

mental boost

anti-aging: skin, hair & eye health

detoxify & manage weight

energy boost

THAI LETTUCE WRAPS
WITH PEANUT DIPPING SAUCE

PEANUT SAUCE:

4g FRESH GINGER, ROUGHLY CHOPPED

125ml WATER

15ml FISH SAUCE (OPTIONAL)

15ml RICE WINE VINEGAR

65g CREAMY PEANUT BUTTER

12g SUGAR

60ml HOISIN SAUCE

1g FRESH CORIANDER LEAVES (OPTIONAL)

LETTUCE WRAPS:

2 LARGE BONELESS, SKINLESS CHICKEN
    BREASTS, COOKED, SLICED INTO THIN STRIPS

10 LARGE ICEBERG LETTUCE LEAVES

115g VERMICELLI RICE NOODLES,
    COOKED AND COOLED

1 LARGE CARROT, PEELED AND SHREDDED

8g FRESH CORIANDER LEAVES,
    ROUGHLY CHOPPED

Place all of the peanut sauce ingredients in the Single Serve Cup and pulse until very smooth. Pour into a small bowl and set aside. On a large serving platter, place the following ingredients in separate sections: chicken strips, iceberg lettuce leaves, rice noodles, shredded carrot and coriander leaves. To assemble, fill the lettuce leaves with equal portions of chicken, noodles, carrots, and coriander. Roll up and serve right away with the peanut dipping sauce. Makes 10 lettuce wraps.

SAUCE: **CAL 135, FAT 7G, SAT FAT 1G, CHOL 0MG, SODIUM 704MG, CARBS 15G, PROTEIN 4G, FIBRE 1G, CALCIUM 15MG, POTASSIUM 129MG**

WRAPS: **CAL 75, FAT 0G, SAT FAT 0G, CHOL 18MG, SODIUM 33MG, CARBS 9G, PROTEIN 8G, FIBRE 1G, CALCIUM 14MG, POTASSIUM 105MG**

anti-inflammatory

immune boost

anti-aging: skin,
hair & eye health

detoxify &
manage weight

digestion

energy boost

DUXELLE CUCUMBER CUPS

450g FRESH CREMINI MUSHROOMS, TRIMMED

1 CLOVE GARLIC, PEELED

1g FRESH THYME LEAVES

2g LEMON ZEST

15ml EXTRA VIRGIN OLIVE OIL

3g SALT

PINCH GROUND BLACK PEPPER

2 SEEDLESS, THIN-SKINNED ENGLISH CUCUMBERS

125ml CRÈME FRAICHE (OR USE SOUR CREAM, IF DESIRED)

PARSLEY FOR GARNISH (OPTIONAL)

Place the mushrooms, garlic, thyme and lemon zest in the 1.1L Processing Bowl and pulse until the mixture is chunky. In a large pan over medium-high heat, sauté the mushroom mixture in the olive oil for about 5 minutes, allowing the excess liquid to cook off. Add salt and pepper and let cool.

Meanwhile, peel the cucumber partially, so it still has strips of skin. Trim the ends off the cucumbers and cut each cucumber into slices 2.5cm thick. Scoop out the center of each slice with a melon baller, forming a cup of flesh. Fill the cucumber cup with 1 teaspoon of the mushroom mixture. Top each with a dollop of crème fraiche and garnish with parsley leaves. Makes 16 appetizers.

CAL 91, FAT 3G, SAT FAT 1G, CHOL 3MG, SODIUM 1216MG,
CARBS 7G, PROTEIN 2G, FIBRE 2G, CALCIUM 18MG, POTASSIUM 277MG

anti-inflammatory

immune boost

mental boost

anti-aging: skin, hair & eye health

digestion

energy boost

MELON CUCUMBER SALSA

½ HONEYDEW MELON, PEELED, ROUGHLY CUT

½ CUCUMBER, PEELED, ROUGHLY CUT

11g FRESH DILL, ROUGHLY CUT

½ RIPE TOMATO, ROUGHLY CUT

½ SWEET ONION, PEELED, ROUGHLY CUT

2ml LEMON JUICE

Place all ingredients in the 1.1L Processing Bowl and pulse a few times until evenly chopped. Makes about 520g.

CAL 21, FAT 0G, SAT FAT 0G, CHOL 0MG, SODIUM 8MG,
CARBS 5G, PROTEIN 0G, FIBRE 0G, CALCIUM 6MG, POTASSIUM 160MG

BACON & CHEDDAR STUFFED BOULE

6 SLICES CRISP COOKED BACON, PLUS MORE FOR GARNISH

¼ RED ONION, PEELED, ROUGHLY CUT

1 SPRIG ROSEMARY, REMOVED FROM STALK, PLUS MORE FOR GARNISH

115g MATURE CHEDDAR CHEESE, CUT INTO 29g STICKS

15ml BALSAMIC VINEGAR

100g LOW FAT PLAIN GREEK YOGURT

250g LOW FAT CREAM CHEESE

1 BOULE SOURDOUGH BREAD (ROUND BREAD LOAF)

Preheat the oven to 180°C/Gas Mark 4.

Place all ingredients, except the bread, in the 1.1L Processing Bowl and pulse until smooth. Slice off the top of the sourdough round and remove most of the bread center, reserving the bread inside. Fill the center of the boule with the dip and cover with the top slice. Wrap in foil and bake for 50 minutes. Unwrap and bake for an additional 10 minutes.

Cut the bread pieces into rough cubes and arrange around the boule. Garnish with additional bacon and rosemary. Serves 8.

CAL 253, FAT 7G, SAT FAT 3G, CHOL 13MG, SODIUM 563MG,
CARBS 33G, PROTEIN 15G, FIBRE 1G, CALCIUM 96MG, POTASSIUM 90MG

immune boost

anti-aging: skin hair & eye health

digestion

energy boost

anti-inflammatory

immune boost

mental boost

relaxation &
stress relief

anti-aging: skin,
hair & eye health

detoxify &
manage weight

energy boost

BLUE CHEESE & WALNUT STUFFED PORTABELLO MUSHROOMS

30g TOASTED WALNUTS

3 LARGE PORTABELLO MUSHROOMS,
   CLEANED AND STEMS REMOVED

15ml EXTRA VIRGIN OLIVE OIL

3g SALT

PINCH GROUND BLACK PEPPER

170g BLUE CHEESE, CRUMBLED

250g LOW FAT CREAM CHEESE, AT ROOM
   TEMPERATURE

45g LOW FAT SOUR CREAM

30ml LOW FAT MILK

Preheat the broiler to High. Place the walnuts in the Single Serve Cup and pulse until chopped. Set aside. Brush the mushrooms with olive oil and place on the broiler pan. Season with salt and pepper. Broil for 5 to 6 minutes, turning once. Remove and set aside to cool.

Place the blue cheese, cream cheese, sour cream and milk in the 1.1L Processing Bowl. Pulse until smooth. Spread the cheese mixture on the broiled mushrooms. Cut each mushroom into 6 wedges. Sprinkle with chopped walnuts and serve right away. Makes 18 appetizers.

CAL 91, FAT 7G, SAT FAT 4G, CHOL 16MG, SODIUM 239MG,
CARBS 2G, PROTEIN 4G, FIBRE 0G, CALCIUM 75MG, POTASSIUM 133MG

anti-inflammatory

mental boost

relaxation & stress relief

anti-aging skin, hair & eye health

detoxify & manage weight

energy boost

CHILLED JUMBO SHRIMP
WITH SWEET CHILI DIPPING SAUCE

450g EXTRA LARGE SHRIMP, COOKED, SHELLED, DEVEINED, WITH TAILS

60ml RICE WINE VINEGAR

30ml FISH SAUCE

60ml HOT WATER

30ml SUGAR

15ml FRESH LIME JUICE

½ CLOVE GARLIC

5g ASIAN RED CHILI PASTE (SUCH AS SAMBAL)

Place the shrimp over ice in a serving bowl and keep well-chilled.

Combine all remaining ingredients in the Single Serve Cup and pulse until smooth. Serve the shrimp with the sauce right away. Chill any leftovers. Serves 3 to 4.

CAL 54, FAT 0G, SAT FAT 0G, CHOL 43MG, SODIUM 753MG,
CARBS 7G, PROTEIN 5G, FIBRE 0G, CALCIUM 16MG, POTASSIUM 78MG

anti-inflammatory

immune boost

mental boost

relaxation & stress relief

anti-aging: skin, hair & eye health

detoxify & manage weight

energy boost

CRUDITES
WITH COOL ARTICHOKE-SPINACH DIP

COOL ARTICHOKE-SPINACH DIP:

**250g LOW FAT CREAM CHEESE, AT ROOM
  TEMPERATURE**

60ml LOW FAT MILK

**400g CAN ARTICHOKE HEARTS IN WATER,
  DRAINED AND ROUGHLY CHOPPED**

**30g FRESH SPINACH LEAVES, WASHED
  AND DRAINED, STEMS REMOVED**

3 SPRING ONIONS, ROUGHLY CUT

15ml FRESH LEMON JUICE

25g PARMESAN CHEESE, GRATED

CRUDITES:

BROCCOLI FLORETS

CARROT STICKS

RED PEPPER STRIPS

CELERY OR JICAMA STICKS

Place the cream cheese and milk in the 1.1L Processing Bowl. Pulse until smooth. Add the remaining ingredients and pulse again until smooth. Spoon into a serving bowl. Serve with the crudités right away or chill until serving. Serves 8.

**CAL 100, FAT 6G, SAT FAT 4G, CHOL 19MG, SODIUM 91MG,
CARBS 6G, PROTEIN 2G, FIBRE 1G, CALCIUM 70MG, POTASSIUM 101MG**

SALSA GUACAMOLE

¼ **RED ONION, PEELED, ROUGHLY CUT**

½ **JALAPEÑO PEPPER, SEEDED, ROUGHLY CUT**

1 **LARGE TOMATO, QUARTERED**

4g **FRESH CORIANDER, LOOSELY PACKED**

½ **YELLOW PEPPER, SEEDED, ROUGHLY CUT**

PINCH RED PEPPER FLAKES

2 **LIMES, JUICED**

2 **RIPE AVOCADOS, PITTED, PEELED, ROUGHLY CUT**

Place all ingredients in the 1.1L Processing Bowl. Pulse quickly three to six times to rough chop or pulse continuously for creamy texture. Makes about 520g.

CAL 125, FAT 10G, SAT FAT 1G, CHOL 0MG, SODIUM 7MG,

CARBS 10G, PROTEIN 2G, FIBRE 5G, CALCIUM 14MG, POTASSIUM 422MG

anti-inflammatory

immune boost

mental boost

relaxation & stress relief

anti-aging skin, hair & eye health

detoxify & manage weight

digestion

anti-inflammatory

immune boost

relaxation & stress relief

anti-aging; skin, hair & eye health

detoxify & manage weight

digestion

energy boost

GREEN GODDESS DIP
WITH TENDER-CRISP GREEN BEANS

200g LOW FAT PLAIN GREEK YOGURT

2 RIPE AVOCADOS, PEELED AND PIT REMOVED

2 SPRING ONIONS, COARSELY CHOPPED

15g FRESH FLAT-LEAF PARSLEY

6g FRESH BASIL LEAVES

5g FRESH TARRAGON LEAVES

45ml FRESH LEMON JUICE

3g SALT

PINCH GROUND BLACK PEPPER

450g FRESH GREEN BEANS, STEAMED AND CHILLED

Place all the ingredients, except the beans, in the 1.1L Processing Bowl and pulse until very smooth. Spoon the dip into a serving bowl and serve right away with the green beans for dipping. Serves 6.

CAL 162, FAT 10G, SAT FAT 2G, CHOL 2MG, SODIUM 219MG,
CARBS 13G, PROTEIN 7G, FIBRE 7G, CALCIUM 86MG, POTASSIUM 505MG

anti-inflammatory

immune boost

mental boost

relaxation & stress relief

anti-aging: skin, hair & eye health

JAPANESE PORK POTSTICKERS WITH SPICY ASIAN DIPPING SAUCE

1 CLOVE GARLIC, PEELED

1cm GINGER, PEELED

2 SPRING ONIONS, ROUGHLY CUT

1 MEDIUM CARROT, PEELED, QUARTERED

70g CABBAGE, FINELY SHREDDED

1 EGG

230g GROUND EXTRA-LEAN PORK

36 GYOZA WRAPPERS (IN THE ASIAN FOODS AISLE)

30ml WATER

15ml RAPESEED OIL

Place the garlic, ginger, onions and carrot in the 1.1L Processing Bowl. Pulse until finely chopped. Place in a large bowl and add the cabbage, egg and ground pork. Toss lightly until combined. In the middle of one wrapper, mound about 2 teaspoons of the filling. Brush the edges of the wrapper with the water and seal the edges to form half-moons.

Heat the oil in a sauté pan over medium-high heat. Place some of the potstickers flat side down, not touching, in the pan and cook until they brown on the bottom. With pan cover in one hand, add 125ml water and immediately cover. Let steam for 5 minutes, checking to add water if needed. Let the water fully evaporate so that the potstickers can crisp up again. Repeat process with remaining potstickers. Serves 18; 2 potstickers per serving.

CAL 53, FAT 2G, SAT FAT 0G, CHOL 6MG, SODIUM 122MG,
CARBS 7G, PROTEIN 2G, FIBRE 0G, CALCIUM 2MG, POTASSIUM 0MG

anti-inflammatory

immune boost

anti-aging: skin,
hair & eye health

detoxify &
manage weight

CRISP CAULIFLOWER
WITH LEMON TAHINI SAUCE

85g TAHINI (SESAME BUTTER)
60ml FRESH LEMON JUICE
2 CLOVES GARLIC, PEELED
30ml EXTRA VIRGIN OLIVE OIL
3g SALT
15ml WATER
1 HEAD FRESH CAULIFLOWER, CUT INTO SMALL FLORETS, CHILLED

Place all ingredients, except the cauliflower, in the 1.1L Processing Bowl and pulse until smooth. Add water as needed to thin the sauce to desired consistency. Place in a serving bowl and surround with the fresh cauliflower for dipping. Serves 4 to 6.

CAL 176, FAT 15G, SAT FAT 2G, CHOL 0MG, SODIUM 36MG,
CARBS 92G, PROTEIN 5G, FIBRE 3G, CALCIUM 48MG, POTASSIUM 377MG

PARMESAN WHOLE WHEAT BREAD CRUMBS

115g PARMESAN CHEESE, CUT INTO 4 PIECES
3g HERBS DE PROVENCE OR ITALIAN SEASONING, TO TASTE
3 SLICES WHOLE GRAIN BREAD, TORN INTO 4 PIECES

Place all ingredients in the 1.1L Processing Bowl and pulse until even crumbs form. Makes about 120g.

CAL 66, FAT 3G, SAT FAT 2G, CHOL 8MG, SODIUM 171MG,
CARBS 6G, PROTEIN 5G, FIBRE 5G, CALCIUM 106MG, POTASSIUM 22MG

detoxify & manage weight

digestion

energy boost

CHAPTER THREE :: COCKTAILS & PARTY DRINKS

BLUEBERRY CAIPIROSKA – P. 65

APRICOT MOJITO CRUSH – P. 63

REFRESHING CUCUMBER & MINT
CHAMPAGNE COCKTAILS – P. 72

CRANBERRY COSMO FREEZE – P. 64

HONEYDEW MELON GIMLET – P. 66

HARD APPLE POMEGRANATE CIDER – P. 71

TROPICAL SUNSET SPARKLER – P. 73

CLASSIC MARGARITA P. 61

CLASSIC MARGARITA

125ml FRESH LIME JUICE

30ml FRESH ORANGE JUICE

30ml FRESH LEMON JUICE

125ml ORANGE LIQUEUR

125ml TEQUILA

12g SUGAR OR AGAVE NECTAR (OPTIONAL)

320-360g ICE CUBES

Place all ingredients in the 1.1L Processing Bowl and pulse until smooth. Taste and add the sugar or nectar if you like a sweeter flavor. Serve immediately. Serves 3-4.

CAL 182, FAT 0G, SAT FAT 0G, CHOL 0MG, SODIUM 1MG,
CARBS 13G, PROTEIN 0G, FIBRE 0G, CALCIUM 9MG, POTASSIUM 107MG

anti-inflammatory

immune boost

mental boost

relaxation &
stress relief

anti-aging: skin,
hair & eye health

energy boost

immune boost

anti-aging: skin, hair & eye heath

SUMMER PEACH BELLINI

2 RIPE PEACHES, PEELED AND PITTED

180ml PEACH SCHNAPPS

310ml PROSECCO, CHILLED

280-320g ICE CUBES

Place all ingredients in the 1.1L Processing Bowl and pulse until icy and smooth. Serve in champagne glasses. Serves 4.

**CAL 292, FAT 0G, SAT FAT 0G, CHOL 0MG, SODIUM 0MG,
CARBS 24G, FIBRE 1G, PROTEIN 0G, CALCIUM 6MG, POTASSIUM 186MG**

immune boost

mental boost

relaxation &
stress relief

APRICOT MOJITO CRUSH

4 RIPE APRICOTS, PEELED AND PITTED

15ml BLACKSTRAP MOLASSES

15ml WARM WATER

6 MINT LEAVES, PLUS EXTRA FOR GARNISH

250ml WHITE RUM

125ml CLUB SODA

280-320g ICE CUBES

Place the apricots, molasses and water in the 1.1L Processing Bowl and pulse until smooth. Spoon equally into 4 glasses and set aside.

Place the remaining ingredients in the 1.1L Processing Bowl and pulse until icy and smooth. Pour over the apricot crush and serve right away. Garnish with mint, if desired. Serves 4.

CAL 192, FAT 0G, SAT FAT 0G, CHOL 0MG, SODIUM 25MG,
CARBS 16G, PROTEIN 0G, FIBRE 1G, CALCIUM 175MG, POTASSIUM 592MG

immune boost

mental boost

anti-aging: skin, hair & eye health

detoxify & manage weight

CRANBERRY COSMO FREEZE

50g FRESH CRANBERRIES, WASHED
125ml CRANBERRY JUICE
60ml TRIPLE SEC
125ml VODKA, CHILLED

In advance, place the cranberries and juice in the 1.1L Processing Bowl and pulse until smooth. Spoon the mixture into ice cube trays and freeze until ice cubes are formed.

Place the cranberry ice cubes and the remaining ingredients in the 1.1L Processing Bowl. Pulse until smooth. Serve right away in chilled martini glasses. Serves 4.

CAL 293, FAT 0G, SAT FAT 0G, CHOL 0MG, SODIUM 18MG,
CARBS 7G, PROTEIN 6G, FIBRE 0G, CALCIUM 0MG, POTASSIUM 26MG

BLUEBERRY CAIPIROSKA

150g FRESH BLUEBERRIES, WASHED

250ml VODKA

320g ICE CUBES

8 LARGE MINT LEAVES FOR GARNISH

Place all ingredients in the 1.1L Processing Bowl and pulse until smooth. Serves 4.

CAL 161, FAT 0G, SAT FAT 0G, CHOL 0MG, SODIUM 1MG,
CARBS 4G, PROTEIN 0G, FIBRE 1G, CALCIUM 2MG, POTASSIUM 23MG

anti-inflammatory

immune boost

mental boost

relaxation & stress relief

anti-aging, skin, hair & eye health

detoxify & manage weight

digestion

energy boost

HONEYDEW MELON GIMLET

170g HONEYDEW MELON, IN CHUNKS
10ml FRESH LIME JUICE
250ml DRY GIN
4 SLICES FRESH LIME (OPTIONAL)
ICE CUBES

Place the melon, juice and gin in the 1.1L Processing Bowl and pulse until smooth. Strain before serving, if desired. Pour over ice cubes and garnish with lime slices. Serves 4.

detoxify &
manage weight

digestion

CAL 146, FAT 0G, SAT FAT 0G, CHOL 0MG, SODIUM 9MG,
CARBS 6G, PROTEIN 1G, FIBRE 1G, CALCIUM 13MG, POTASSIUM 174MG

anti-inflammatory

immune booster

relaxation &
stress relief

anti-aging: skin,
hair & eye health

RIPE PLUM PARADISE

1 FRESH, RIPE PLUM, PITTED
125ml PLUM BRANDY
30ml ORANGE LIQUEUR
250ml DARK RUM
ICE CUBES

Place the plum, brandy, liqueur and rum in the 1.1L Processing Bowl and pulse until smooth.
Pour over the ice cubes before serving. Serves 3 to 4.

CAL 231, FAT 0G, SAT FAT 0G, CHOL 0MG, SODIUM 1MG,
CARBS 7G, PROTEIN 4G, FIBRE 0G, CALCIUM 2MG, POTASSIUM 55MG

anti-inflammatory

immune boost

mental boost

relaxation &
stress relief

anti-aging: skin,
hair & eye health

PERFECT PINA COLADA

250ml FRESH PINEAPPLE JUICE
225g PINEAPPLE SORBET
125ml LIGHT COCONUT MILK
125ml WHITE RUM
PINEAPPLE WEDGES (OPTIONAL)
ICE CUBES

Place all the ingredients, except the pineapple wedges, in the 1.1L Processing Bowl and pulse until smooth. Pour over ice cubes into cocktail glasses and garnish with a wedge of fresh pineapple. Serves 4.

CAL 294, FAT 3G, SAT FAT 0G, CHOL 0MG, SODIUM 13MG,
CARBS 35G, PROTEIN 0G, FIBRE 0G, CALCIUM 9MG, POTASSIUM 90MG

mental boost

SAIGON BY NIGHT

450g VANILLA ICE CREAM

125ml COLD ESPRESSO COFFEE

60ml COFFEE LIQUEUR

Place the ingredients in the 1.1L Processing Bowl and pulse until smooth. Serves 4.

anti-aging, skin
hair & eye health

CAL 249, FAT 11G, SAT FAT 7G, CHOL 78MG, SODIUM 54MG,

CARBS 27G, PROTEIN 4G, FIBRE 2G, CALCIUM 113MG, POTASSIUM 158MG

anti-inflammatory

immune boost

relaxation &
stress relief

detoxify &
manage weight

digestion

energy boost

GRANNY'S APPLE MARTINI

1 GRANNY SMITH APPLE, PEELED, CORED, ROUGHLY CUT
250ml VODKA, CHILLED
90ml CALVADOS
ICE CUBES
APPLE PEEL FOR GARNISH (OPTIONAL)

Place the apple in the 1.1L Processing Bowl and pulse until smooth. Add the remaining ingredients and pulse again. Strain before serving, if desired.

Fill 4 martini glasses with ice cubes and pour the apple martinis equally into each. Garnish with apple peel, if desired. Serve immediately. Serves 4.

CAL 248, FAT 0G, SAT FAT 0G, CHOL 0MG, SODIUM 2MG,
CARBS 10G, PROTEIN 0G, FIBRE 2G, CALCIUM 5MG, POTASSIUM 82MG

HARD APPLE POMEGRANATE CIDER

1 RIPE RED DELICIOUS APPLE, CORED, ROUGHLY CUT
250ml APPLE BRANDY
125ml POMEGRANATE JUICE
250ml APPLE CIDER
2 CINNAMON STICKS

Place the apple in the 1.1L Processing Bowl and pulse until smooth. Add the brandy, juice and cider and pulse again until smooth. Strain, if desired.

Pour the cider into a large saucepan and add the cinnamon sticks. Heat on medium-low until simmering, stirring occasionally. Remove the cinnamon sticks and ladle into four heatproof mugs. Serve right away. Serves 4.

CAL 184, FAT 0G, SAT FAT 0G, CHOL 0MG, SODIUM 30MG,
CARBS 32G, PROTEIN 0G, FIBRE 0G, CALCIUM 61MG, POTASSIUM 339MG

anti-inflammatory

immune boost

relaxation & stress relief

anti-aging: skin, hair & eye health

detoxify & manage weight

digestion

energy boost

anti-inflammatory

immune boost

anti-aging: skin, hair & eye health

digestion

energy boost

REFRESHING CUCUMBER & MINT
CHAMPAGNE COCKTAILS

1 SMALL CUCUMBER, PEELED, QUARTERED

6 LARGE MINT LEAVES

40g RAW, UNFILTERED HONEY

60ml MIDORI

375ml DRY CHAMPAGNE, CHILLED

Place the cucumber, mint leaves and honey in the 1.1L Processing Bowl and pulse until smooth. Add the Midori and champagne and pulse again. Strain and pour into champagne glasses. Serve right away. Serves 4.

CAL 137, FAT 0G, SAT FAT 0G, CHOL 0MG, SODIUM 1MG,
CARBS 8G, PROTEIN 1G, FIBRE 1G, CALCIUM 7MG, POTASSIUM 71MG

TROPICAL SUNSET SPARKLER

400g ICE CUBES

125ml ORANGE JUICE

125ml PINEAPPLE JUICE

375ml PROSECCO OR CHAMPAGNE

60ml GRENADINE

4 FRESH SWEET CHERRIES

Place the ice cubes in the 1.1L Processing Bowl. Pulse until completely smooth. Divide the powdered ice evenly among four cocktail glasses.

Place the orange juice, pineapple juice, and Prosecco in the 1.1L Processing Bowl and pulse until blended. Pour equally over the ice. Do not stir or mix. Drizzle 1 tablespoon of grenadine over the top of each cocktail and top with a cherry.

CAL 262, FAT 0G, SAT FAT 0G, CHOL 0MG, SODIUM 10MG, CARBS 45G, PROTEIN 2G, FIBRE 0G, CALCIUM 32MG, POTASSIUM 422MG

anti-inflammatory

immune boost

mental boost

relaxation & stress relief

anti-aging skin, hair & eye health

energy boost

immune boost

mental boost

anti-aging: skin, hair & eye health

detoxify & manage weight

digestion

energy boost

BLACKBERRY GIN TWIST

250ml GIN

125ml GINGER BEER

145g FRESH, RIPE BLACKBERRIES, RINSED

280-320g ICE CUBES

BLACKBERRIES FOR GARNISH (OPTIONAL)

Place all ingredients, except the garnish, in the 1.1L Processing Bowl and pulse until smooth. Spoon into cocktail glasses and garnish each with a blackberry. Serve right away. Serves 4.

**CAL 191, FAT 0G, SAT FAT 0G, CHOL 0MG, SODIUM 1MG,
CARBS 17G, PROTEIN 0G, FIBRE 2G, CALCIUM 8MG, POTASSIUM 47MG**

HARD RASPBERRY & MINT LEMONADE

250ml VODKA

250ml CLUB SODA

125ml LEMONADE

60g FRESH RASPBERRIES, RINSED

16g ICING SUGAR

4 MINT LEAVES

 ICE CUBES

Place all the ingredients, except the ice cubes, in the 1.1L Processing Bowl and pulse until blended. Fill 4 cocktail glasses with ice cubes and pour the lemonade over each. Serve right away. Serves 4.

CAL 190, FAT 0G, SAT FAT 0G, CHOL 0MG, SODIUM 10MG, CARBS 12G, PROTEIN 0G, FIBRE 0G, CALCIUM 5MG, POTASSIUM 35MG

anti-inflammatory

immune boost

mental boost

anti-aging: skin, hair & eye health

detoxify & manage weight

energy boost

CHAPTER FOUR :: SMOOTHIES & JUICES

CARROT APPLE REFRESHER – P.105

BLUEBERRY BLAST – P. 85

GARDEN VEGGIES IN A GLASS– P. 106

PEANUT BUTTER CHOCOLATE SMOOTHIE – P. 92

WATERMELON & LIME SMOOTHIE – P. 110

ALMOND & DARK MOLASSES DREAM – P. 108

STRAWBERRY BANANA SMOOTHIE

125ml APPLE JUICE

120g LOW FAT PLAIN YOGURT

115g FRESH STRAWBERRIES, STEMMED AND HULLED

½ BANANA, PEELED

100-120g ICE CUBES

Place all ingredients in the Single Serve Cup. Pulse until smooth. Serve right away.

CAL 224, FAT 2G, SAT FAT 1G, CHOL 7MG, SODIUM 19MG,
CARBS 45G, PROTEIN 8G, FIBRE 4G, CALCIUM 250MG, POTASSIUM 664MG

anti-inflammatory

immune boost

mental boost

relaxation & stress relief

anti-aging, skin, hair & eye health

detoxify & manage weight

digestion

energy boost

anti-inflammatory

immune boost

mental boost

relaxation &
stress relief

anti-aging: skin,
hair & eye health

detoxify &
manage weight

digestion

energy boost

EMERALD GREEN ELIXIR

125ml WHITE GRAPE JUICE

½ SMALL BANANA, PEELED

15g BABY SPINACH LEAVES

1 KIWI, PEELED

15g RAW, UNFILTERED HONEY

100-120g ICE CUBES

Place all ingredients in the Single Serve Cup and pulse until smooth. Serve right away.

CAL 220, FAT 0G, SAT FAT 0G, CHOL 0MG, SODIUM 25MG,
CARBS 51G, PROTEIN 2G, FIBRE 4G, CALCIUM 44MG, POTASSIUM 535MG

BLUEBERRY BLAST

125ml WHITE GRAPE JUICE

120g LOW FAT PLAIN YOGURT

½ BANANA, PEELED

75g FRESH OR FROZEN WILD BLUEBERRIES, RINSED

160g ICE CUBES

Place all ingredients in the Single Serve Cup and pulse until smooth.

CAL 252, FAT 2G, SAT FAT 1G, CHOL 7MG, SODIUM 97MG,
CARBS 54G, PROTEIN 8G, FIBRE 4G, CALCIUM 231MG, POTASSIUM 556MG

anti-inflammatory

immune boost

mental boost

relaxation & stress relief

anti-aging skin, hair & eye health

detoxify & manage weight

digestion

energy boost

anti-inflammatory

immune boost

mental boost

relaxation &
stress relief

anti-aging: skin,
hair & eye health

detoxify &
manage weight

digestion

energy boost

POMEGRANATE POWER SMOOTHIE

120g LOW FAT PLAIN YOGURT

125ml POMEGRANATE JUICE

20g FROZEN BLUEBERRIES

20g RAW, UNFILTERED HONEY

Place all ingredients in the Single Serve Cup and pulse until smooth.

CAL 223, FAT 2G, SAT FAT 1G, CHOL 7MG, SODIUM 118MG,

CARBS 50G, PROTEIN 7G, FIBRE 2G, CALCIUM 239MG, POTASSIUM 497MG

MANGO LASSI

80g MANGO CHUNKS, FROZEN

120g LOW FAT PLAIN YOGURT

60ml MANGO JUICE OR MILK

8g RAW, UNFILTERED HONEY

PINCH GROUND CARDAMOM

Place all ingredients in the Single Serve Cup and pulse until smooth.

CAL 225, FAT 2G, SAT FAT 1G, CHOL 7MG, SODIUM 92MG,
CARBS 47G, PROTEIN 6G, FIBRE 2G, CALCIUM 233MG, POTASSIUM 429MG

immune boost

mental boost

anti-aging, skin,
hair & eye health

digestion

energy boost

anti-inflammatory

relaxation & stress relief

anti-aging: skin, hair & eye health

digestion

energy boost

AVOCADO SHAKE

½ RIPE AVOCADO, PITTED AND PEELED

125ml LOW FAT MILK

20g RAW, UNFILTERED HONEY

160g ICE CUBES

Place all ingredients in the Single Serve Cup and pulse until smooth. Serve at once.

CAL 306, FAT 16G, SAT FAT 3G, CHOL 6MG, SODIUM 483MG,

CARBS 12G, PROTEIN 16G, FIBRE 7G, CALCIUM 82MG, POTASSIUM 595MG

DANDY GREEN MACHINE

125ml APPLE JUICE

20g SWISS CHARD, RINSED, ROUGHLY TORN

½ BANANA, PEELED

20g GOJI BERRIES

120-160g ICE CUBES

Place the ingredients in the Single Serve Cup and pulse until smooth. Serve right away.

**CAL 220, FAT 1G, SAT FAT 0G, CHOL 0MG, SODIUM 115MG,
CARBS 54G, PROTEIN 5G, FIBRE 6G, CALCIUM 102MG, POTASSIUM 399MG**

anti-inflammatory

mental boost

relaxation &
stress relief

digestion

energy boost

anti-inflammatory

immune boost

mental boost

relaxation & stress relief

anti-aging: skin, hair & eye health

detoxify & manage weight

digestion

energy boost

SWEET CHERRY SMOOTHIE

125ml LOW FAT MILK

120g LOW FAT VANILLA YOGURT

90g FRESH SWEET CHERRIES, PITTED (OR USE FROZEN CHERRIES, IF DESIRED)

½ BANANA, PEELED

100-120g ICE CUBES

Place all ingredients in the Single Serve Cup and pulse until smooth.

CAL 239, FAT 2G, SAT FAT 2G, CHOL 10MG, SODIUM 134MG,
CARBS 46G, PROTEIN 10G, FIBRE 12G, CALCIUM 344MG, POTASSIUM 808MG

KALE & DATE SMOOTHIE

180ml FRESH ORANGE JUICE
120g NONFAT VANILLA YOGURT
½ BANANA, PEELED
30g FRESH KALE, TIGHTLY PACKED
1 DATE, PITTED
100-120g ICE CUBES

Place all ingredients in the Single Serve Cup. Pulse until smooth. Serve right away.

CAL 363, FAT 0G, SAT FAT 0G, CHOL 3MG, SODIUM 101MG,
CARBS 87G, PROTEIN 9G, FIBRE 6G, CALCIUM 299MG, POTASSIUM 1052MG

anti-inflammatory

immune boost

mental boost

relaxation &
stress relief

anti-aging skin,
hair & eye health

energy boost

anti-inflammatory

immune boost

anti-aging: skin, hair & eye health

digestion

energy boost

PEANUT BUTTER CHOCOLATE SMOOTHIE

60ml LOW FAT MILK

30g CREAMY PEANUT BUTTER

130g LOW FAT VANILLA FROZEN YOGURT

30g DARK CHOCOLATE

Place all ingredients in the Single Serve Cup and pulse until smooth. Serve right away.

CAL 395, FAT 18G, SAT FAT 7G, CHOL 5MG, SODIUM 239MG,

CARBS 61G, PROTEIN 15G, FIBRE 10G, CALCIUM 438MG, POTASSIUM 204MG

GALA APPLE CELEBRATION

125ml APPLE JUICE

½ RIPE GALA APPLE, CORED, ROUGHLY CUT

18g COLLARD GREENS, RINSED, RIBS REMOVED

120g NONFAT PLAIN YOGURT

PINCH GROUND CARDAMOM

100-120g ICE CUBES

Place all ingredients in the Single Serve Cup and pulse until smooth. Strain before serving, if desired.

**CAL 211, FAT 0G, SAT FAT 0G, CHOL 0MG, SODIUM 97MG,
CARBS 47G, PROTEIN 7G, FIBRE 4G, CALCIUM 216MG, POTASSIUM 195MG**

anti-inflammatory

immune boost

relaxation &
stress relief

detoxify &
manage weight

digestion

energy boost

anti-inflammatory

immune boost

mental boost

relaxation &
stress relief

detoxify &
manage weight

digestion

energy boost

CARROT PROTEIN POWER

125ml APPLE JUICE

½ SMALL CARROT, ROUGHLY CUT

¼ SMALL RIPE GRANNY SMITH APPLE

½ BANANA, PEELED

15g WHEY PROTEIN POWDER

100-120g ICE CUBES

Place all ingredients in the Single Serve Cup and pulse until smooth. Strain before serving, if desired.

**CAL 271, FAT 2G, SAT FAT 1G, CHOL 60MG, SODIUM 93MG,
CARBS 46G, PROTEIN 19G, FIBRE 5G, CALCIUM 17MG, POTASSIUM 640MG**

VITAMIN C CUCUMBER BLAST

1 GRAPEFRUIT, PEELED AND QUARTERED

1 ORANGE, PEELED AND QUARTERED

¼ CUCUMBER, PEELED

40-60g ICE CUBES

Place all ingredients in the Single Serve Cup. Pulse until smooth.

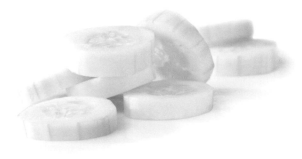

CAL 150, FAT 0G, SAT FAT 0G, CHOL 0MG, SODIUM 1MG,

CARBS 38G, PROTEIN 3G, FIBRE 6G, CALCIUM 90MG, POTASSIUM 661MG

anti-inflammatory

immune boost

mental boost

relaxation & stress relief

anti-aging: skin, hair & eye health

detoxify & manage weight

digestion

energy boost

anti-inflammatory

immune boost

relaxation & stress relief

detoxify & manage weight

digestion

energy boost

DETOX ANTIOXIDANT JUICE

1 APPLE, CORED AND QUARTERED

½ STALK CELERY, QUARTERED

250ml GREEN TEA, COOLED

½ LEMON, JUICED

40-60g ICE CUBES

Place the ingredients in the Single Serve Cup. Pulse until smooth.

**CAL 109, FAT 0G, SAT FAT 0G, CHOL 0MG, SODIUM 6MG,
CARBS 28G, PROTEIN 3G, FIBRE 4G, CALCIUM 13MG, POTASSIUM 263MG**

RAINBOW JUICE

4 LARGE STRAWBERRIES, STEMMED

40g PINEAPPLE, ROUGHLY CUT

20g GREENS (USE SPINACH, COLLARD GREENS, DANDELION GREENS OR KALE)

80ml WATER

40-60g ICE CUBES

Place all ingredients in the Single Serve Cup. Pulse until smooth.

CAL 53, FAT 0G, SAT FAT 0G, CHOL 0MG, SODIUM 14MG,
CARBS 12G, PROTEIN 1G, FIBRE 3G, CALCIUM 58MG, POTASSIUM 268MG

anti-inflammatory

immune boost

mental boost

relaxation &
stress relief

anti-aging, skin,
hair & eye health

detoxify &
manage weight

energy boost

anti-inflammatory

immune boost

mental boost

relaxation & stress relief

anti-aging: skin, hair & eye health

detoxify & manage weight

energy boost

VEGGIE FUSION

⅛ CUCUMBER, CUT INTO 2 WEDGES, 7.5CM IN LENGTH

2 BABY CARROTS

1 SMALL STALK CELERY, CUT IN HALF TO 7.5cm IN LENGTH

15g SPINACH LEAVES, LIGHTLY PACKED

¼ RIPE TOMATO

7 RED OR GREEN SEEDLESS GRAPES

40-50g WATERMELON, CUT INTO CHUNKS

3 TO 4 ORANGE SLICES, PEELED

2 FRESH STRAWBERRIES (OR USE FROZEN)

40-60g ICE CUBES

Place all the ingredients in the Single Serve Cup. Pulse until smooth.

CAL 42, FAT 0G, SAT FAT 0G, CHOL 0MG, SODIUM 32MG,
CARBS 19G, PROTEIN 1G, FIBRE 2G, CALCIUM 63MG, POTASSIUM 583MG

SUMMER BERRY SENSATION

125ml APPLE JUICE

120g LOW FAT VANILLA FROZEN YOGURT

40g FROZEN RASPBERRIES

40g FROZEN BLUEBERRIES

40g FROZEN STRAWBERRIES

Place all ingredients in the Single Serve Cup and pulse until smooth. Serve right away.

**CAL 266, FAT 3G, SAT FAT 2G, CHOL 10MG, SODIUM 66MG,
CARBS 55G, PROTEIN 11G, FIBRE 5G, CALCIUM 202MG, POTASSIUM 173MG**

anti-inflammatory

immune boost

mental boost

anti-aging: skin, hair & eye health

detoxify & manage weight

digestion

energy boost

mental boost

relaxation &
stress relief

anti-aging: skin,
hair & eye health

detoxify &
manage weight

digestion

energy boost

GREEN PEAR SMOOTHIE

15g BABY SPINACH LEAVES
½ RIPE BARTLETT PEAR, PEELED AND CORED
½ BANANA, PEELED
100-120g ICE CUBES

Place all ingredients in the Single Serve Cup and pulse until smooth. Strain before serving, if desired. Serve right away.

**CAL 104, FAT 0G, SAT FAT 0G, CHOL 0MG, SODIUM 14MG,
CARBS 27G, PROTEIN 1G, FIBRE 5G, CALCIUM 26MG, POTASSIUM 394MG**

PINEAPPLE PAPAYA SMOOTHIE

60ml PAPAYA JUICE

80g FRESH PINEAPPLE, CUT INTO CHUNKS

70g FRESH PAPAYA

120g LOW FAT VANILLA YOGURT

100-120g ICE CUBES

Place all ingredients in the Single Serve Cup and pulse until smooth.

CAL 191, FAT 1G, SAT FAT 1G, CHOL 5MG, SODIUM 79MG,
CARBS 41G, PROTEIN 5G, FIBRE 2G, CALCIUM 192MG, POTASSIUM 515MG

anti-inflammatory

immune boost

relaxation & stress relief

anti-aging, skin, hair & eye health

detoxify & manage weight

digestion

anti-inflammatory

immune boost

mental boost

relaxation & stress relief

anti-aging: skin, hair & eye health

detoxify & manage weight

energy boost

FRESH CITRUS SQUEEZE

60ml FRESH ORANGE JUICE

115g FRESH RED GRAPEFRUIT, PEELED, SEGMENTED

90g FRESH ORANGE, PEELED, SEGMENTED

120g LOW FAT PLAIN YOGURT

3g ICING SUGAR

120g ICE CUBES

Place all ingredients in the Single Serve Cup and pulse until smooth. Serve right away.

CAL 201, FAT 1G, SAT FAT 1G, CHOL 5MG, SODIUM 73MG,
CARBS 45G, PROTEIN 2G, FIBRE 2G, CALCIUM 196MG, POTASSIUM 521MG

QUICK ORANGESICLE

175g LOW FAT VANILLA FROZEN YOGURT
60ml ORANGE JUICE
90g FRESH ORANGE, PEELED, SEGMENTED

Place all ingredients in the Single Serve Cup and pulse until smooth. Serve right away.

CAL 287, FAT 0G, SAT FAT 0G, CHOL 4MG, SODIUM 122MG,
CARBS 64G, PROTEIN 1G, FIBRE 3G, CALCIUM 76MG, POTASSIUM 763MG

anti-inflammatory

immune boost

mental boost

relaxation &
stress relief

anti-aging: skin,
hair & eye health

energy boost

anti-inflammatory

immune boost

mental boost

relaxation &
stress relief

anti-aging; skin,
hair & eye heath

energy boost

PUMPKIN GINGER SMOOTHIE

120g PUMPKIN PUREE

125ml ORANGE JUICE

120g LOW FAT VANILLA YOGURT

PINCH FRESH GINGER

PINCH GROUND CINNAMON (OPTIONAL)

RAW, UNFILTERED HONEY (OPTIONAL)

100-120g ICE CUBES

Place all ingredients in the Single Serve Cup and pulse until smooth.

**CAL 364, FAT 0G, SAT FAT 0G, CHOL 4MG, SODIUM 403MG,
CARBS 84G, PROTEIN 3G, FIBRE 11G, CALCIUM 72MG, POTASSIUM 705MG**

CARROT APPLE REFRESHER

125ml CARROT JUICE

½ SMALL CARROT, PEELED, ROUGHLY CUT

½ SMALL RIPE GRANNY SMITH APPLE, PEELED, ROUGHLY CUT

60g LOW FAT PLAIN YOGURT

8g RAW, UNFILTERED HONEY (OR TO TASTE)

PINCH GROUND CLOVES

100-120g ICE CUBES

Place all ingredients in the Single Serve Cup and pulse until smooth.

**CAL 183, FAT 0G, SAT FAT 0G, CHOL 2MG, SODIUM 93MG,
CARBS 26G, PROTEIN 1G, FIBRE 3G, CALCIUM 41MG, POTASSIUM 388MG**

anti-inflammatory

immune boost

mental boost

relaxation &
stress relief

anti-aging; skin,
hair & eye health

detoxify &
manage weight

digestion

energy boost

anti-inflammatory

immune booster

mental boost

relaxation &
stress relief

detoxify &
manage weight

digestion

energy boost

GARDEN VEGGIES IN A GLASS

125ml APPLE JUICE
½ SMALL RIPE TOMATO, PEELED, CUT IN HALF
½ INNER STALK CELERY, WITH LEAVES
4g FRESH FLAT-LEAF PARSLEY
½ SPRING ONION, ROUGHLY CUT
PINCH SALT
PINCH GROUND BLACK PEPPER

Place all ingredients in the Single Serve Cup and pulse until smooth. Strain before serving, if desired.

**CAL 78, FAT 0G, SAT FAT 0G, CHOL 0MG, SODIUM 165MG,
CARBS 16G, PROTEIN 1G, FIBRE 2G, CALCIUM 18MG, POTASSIUM 332MG**

RED GRAPE SQUEEZE

90g FROZEN, SEEDLESS RED GRAPES

125ml WHITE GRAPE JUICE

120g LOW FAT VANILLA YOGURT

Place all ingredients in the Single Serve Cup and pulse until smooth.

CAL 192, FAT 0G, SAT FAT 0G, CHOL 2MG, SODIUM 28MG,
CARBS 29G, PROTEIN 0G, FIBRE 0G, CALCIUM 8MG, POTASSIUM 319MG

immune boost

anti-aging, skin, hair & eye health

detoxify & manage weight

energy boost

anti-inflammatory

immune boost

relaxation &
stress relief

anti-aging: skin,
hair & eye health

energy boost

ALMOND & DARK MOLASSES DREAM

60ml ALMOND MILK

5ml BLACKSTRAP MOLASSES

225g LOW FAT VANILLA FROZEN YOGURT

1ml PURE ALMOND ESSENCE (OPTIONAL)

Place all ingredients in the Single Serve Cup and pulse until smooth.

CAL 288, FAT 7G, SAT FAT 4G, CHOL 30MG, SODIUM 179MG,

CARBS 58G, PROTEIN 6G, FIBRE 0G, CALCIUM 422MG, POTASSIUM 543MG

GREEN TEA FREEZE

125ml GREEN TEA, COOLED

175g LOW FAT VANILLA FROZEN YOGURT

PINCH GROUND NUTMEG

PINCH GROUND CARDAMOM

100-120g ICE CUBES

Place all ingredients in the Single Serve Cup and pulse until smooth.

**CAL 240, FAT 6G, SAT FAT 4G, CHOL 30MG, SODIUM 130MG,
CARBS 44G, PROTEIN 6G, FIBRE 0G, CALCIUM 200MG**

anti-inflammatory

immune boost

mental boost

anti-aging, skin,
hair & eye health

digestion

energy boost

immune boost

mental boost

anti-aging: skin, hair & eye health

detoxify & manage weight

energy boost

WATERMELON & LIME SMOOTHIE

60ml WHITE GRAPE JUICE

150g SEEDLESS WATERMELON CHUNKS, FROZEN

1g LIME ZEST (OPTIONAL)

8g RAW, UNFILTERED HONEY (OPTIONAL)

Place all ingredients in the Single Serve Cup and pulse until smooth. Serve right away.

CAL 141, FAT 0G, SAT FAT 0G, CHOL 0MG, SODIUM 7MG,

CARBS 37G, PROTEIN 1G, FIBRE 0G, CALCIUM 10MG, POTASSIUM 148MG

MOCHA FREEZE

125ml STRONG COFFEE, COOLED

85g LOW FAT CHOCOLATE FROZEN YOGURT

30g DARK CHOCOLATE

100-120g ICE CUBES

Place all ingredients in the Single Serve Cup and pulse until smooth. Serve right away.

**CAL 318, FAT 13G, SAT FAT 7G, CHOL 17MG, SODIUM 85MG,
CARBS 47G, PROTEIN 7G, FIBRE 5G, CALCIUM 137MG, POTASSIUM 0MG**

anti-inflammatory

mental boost

anti-aging, skin,
hair & eye health

energy boost

CHAPTER FIVE :: SOUPS & SALADS

COOL SUMMERTIME CORN & RED PEPPER SOUP – P. 121

BOK CHOY SALAD WITH CASHEW DRESSING – P. 136

ASIAN SHRIMP SLAW WITH GINGER SESAME VINAIGRETTE – P. 139

DUO TOMATO GAZPACHO – P. 125

ISLAND BUTTERNUT SQUASH SOUP – P. 119

anti-inflammatory

immune boost

anti-aging: skin, hair & eye health

detoxify & manage weight

digestion

ISLAND BUTTERNUT SQUASH SOUP

3 CLOVES GARLIC, PEELED

10g FRESH GINGER, PEELED

1 JALAPEÑO PEPPER, SEEDED

1 MEDIUM YELLOW ONION, PEELED, ROUGHLY CUT

2kg BUTTERNUT SQUASH, COOKED, CUBED AND COOLED

750ml SODIUM-REDUCED CHICKEN OR VEGETABLE BROTH

6g SALT (OR TO TASTE)

10g BROWN SUGAR (OPTIONAL)

Place the garlic, ginger, pepper and onion in the 1.1L Processing Bowl and pulse until finely chopped. Set aside.

Working in batches, pulse the butternut squash in the 1.1L Processing Bowl and add broth to create a pourable puree. Pour the pureed squash into a large saucepot and add the chopped vegetables. Repeat with the remaining squash. Slowly add the remaining broth, whisking together to combine. Season with salt and sugar as desired. Heat on medium until simmering and ready to serve, about 8 minutes. Serves 4.

**CAL 70, FAT 0G, SAT FAT 0G, CHOL 0MG, SODIUM 999MG,
CARBS 15G, PROTEIN 3G, FIBRE 3G, CALCIUM 65MG, POTASSIUM 518MG**

anti-inflammatory

immune boost

mental boost

relaxation &
stress relief

anti-aging: skin,
hair & eye health

detoxify &
manage weight

ROASTED VEGETABLE BISQUE

1.5kg ROASTED ROOT VEGETABLES (BROCCOLI, ASPARAGUS, SQUASH, SWEET POTATO, CAULIFLOWER, ETC.), COOLED

3g FRESH CHIVES

4g FLAT-LEAF PARSLEY

750ml SODIUM-REDUCED CHICKEN OR VEGETABLE BROTH, DIVIDED

125ml LOW FAT MILK (OR CREAM, IF DESIRED)

6g SALT (OR TO TASTE)

2g GROUND BLACK PEPPER

Place about one-third of the vegetables and herbs in the 1.1L Processing Bowl and add one-half cup of broth. Pulse until pureed and smooth. Spoon the puree into a saucepot and repeat with the remaining roasted vegetables and herbs.

Add the remaining broth and milk, mixing well, and heat on medium until just simmering. Season with salt and pepper to taste, and continue simmering for about 10 minutes. Serves 4.

CAL 115, FAT 1G, SAT FAT 0G, CHOL 1MG, SODIUM 886MG,
CARBS 24G, PROTEIN 11G, FIBRE 6G, CALCIUM 101MG, POTASSIUM 741MG

COOL SUMMERTIME CORN & RED PEPPER SOUP

½ MEDIUM YELLOW ONION, PEELED, ROUGHLY CUT

3 JARRED ROASTED RED PEPPERS

850g CORN EARS, DRAINED, DIVIDED

500ml VEGETABLE BROTH, DIVIDED

230g LOW FAT SOUR CREAM

1g FRESH CORIANDER LEAVES

Place the onion, red peppers and half of the corn in the 1.1L Processing Bowl and pulse until finely chopped. Add one-half of the vegetable broth and pulse again.

Pour the mixture into a large serving bowl and add the remaining corn, broth, sour cream and coriander. Stir lightly until well-mixed and serve right away or chill until serving. Serves 4.

**CAL 213, FAT 8G, SAT FAT 4G, CHOL 20MG, SODIUM 836MG,
CARBS 37G, PROTEIN 6G, FIBRE 4G, CALCIUM 90MG, POTASSIUM 415MG**

anti-inflammatory

immune boost

relaxation &
stress relief

detoxify &
manage weight

digestion

energy boost

immune boost

mental boost

anti-aging: skin, hair & eye health

detoxify & manage weight

digestion

energy boost

WATERMELON MINT SOUP

530g WATERMELON, CUT INTO 2.5cm PIECES

12g SUGAR

1 LEMON, JUICED

8 MINT LEAVES

1 SLICE FRESH GINGER, PEELED

30ml SPARKLING WATER

Place all ingredients in the 1.1L Processing Bowl and pulse to blend until smooth. Serves 4.

CAL 52, FAT 0G, SAT FAT 0G, CHOL 0MG, SODIUM 5MG,

CARBS 13G, PROTEIN 1G, FIBRE 0G, CALCIUM 10MG, POTASSIUM 151MG

SPICED CARROT APPLE SOUP
WITH TOASTED HAZELNUTS

260g CARROTS, PEELED, ROUGHLY CUT

1 MEDIUM RIPE GALA APPLE, PEELED, ROUGHLY CUT

5mm PIECE FRESH GINGER, PEELED

3g GROUND CINNAMON

750ml REDUCED-SODIUM CHICKEN OR VEGETABLE BROTH

60g HAZELNUTS, SKINS REMOVED

15g BUTTER

Place the carrots in the 1.1L Processing Bowl and pulse until finely chopped. Spoon the carrots into a saucepot and set aside. Place the apple, ginger and cinnamon in the Bowl and pulse until finely chopped. Add the mixture to the carrots in the saucepot. Add the broth to the carrot/apple mixture and heat on medium until warm and simmering, about 8 minutes.

Meanwhile, place the hazelnuts in the Bowl and pulse until chopped. Remove and sauté the nuts in the butter on medium heat until lightly toasted and fragrant, about 2 minutes. To serve, ladle the warm soup into bowls and top with the toasted hazelnuts. Serves 4.

**CAL 132, FAT 7G, SAT FAT 2G, CHOL 8MG, SODIUM 481MG,
CARBS 14G, PROTEIN 4G, FIBRE 4G, CALCIUM 47MG, POTASSIUM 457MG**

anti-inflammatory

immune boost

mental boost

relaxation & stress relief

anti-aging: skin, hair & eye health

detoxify & manage weight

digestion

energy boost

anti-inflammatory

immune boost

mental boost

detoxify & manage weight

digestion

energy boost

SPICY BLACK BEAN SOUP

800g BLACK BEANS, DRAINED

1 JALAPEÑO PEPPER, SEEDED, ROUGHLY CUT

1 RIPE TOMATO, ROUGHLY CUT

½ LIME, JUICED

¼ WHITE ONION, PEELED, ROUGHLY CUT

2 CLOVES GARLIC, PEELED

¼ RED PEPPER, SEEDED, ROUGHLY CUT

4g FRESH CORIANDER

SALT AND PEPPER TO TASTE

Place all of the ingredients in the 1.1L Processing Bowl and pulse until smooth. Heat briefly or serve at room temperature. Serves 4.

CAL 184, FAT 1G, SAT FAT 0G, CHOL 0MG, SODIUM 696MG,
CARBS 37G, PROTEIN 13G, FIBRE 12G, CALCIUM 98MG, POTASSIUM 67MG

anti-inflammatory

immune boost

mental boost

detoxify &
manage weight

DUO TOMATO GAZPACHO

1 SLICE STALE WHITE BREAD, ROUGHLY TORN

6 PLUM TOMATOES, HALVED

1 MEDIUM SEEDLESS CUCUMBER, PEELED AND QUARTERED

1 BELL PEPPER, CORED AND SEEDED, QUARTERED

1 CLOVE GARLIC, PEELED

30ml RED WINE VINEGAR

6g SALT (OR TO TASTE)

1g GROUND BLACK PEPPER

250ml TOMATO JUICE (PLUS 250ml, TO TASTE)

Pulse the bread in the 1.1L Processing Bowl until crumbed. Place in a large serving bowl. Place 3 tomatoes in the Bowl and pulse until smooth. Pour into the serving bowl with the crumbs. Repeat with the remaining tomatoes. Pulse the pepper and garlic and add to the tomatoes and crumbs.

Add the vinegar, salt and pepper to taste, plus the tomato juice to taste. Stir well and chill until serving. Serves 4.

CAL 55, FAT 0G, SAT FAT 0G, CHOL 0MG, SODIUM 954MG,
CARBS 12G, PROTEIN 3G, FIBRE 2G, CALCIUM 35MG, POTASSIUM 467MG

immune boost

relaxation & stress relief

anti-aging; skin, hair & eye health

detoxify & manage weight

energy boost

SPRING ASPARAGUS SOUP
WITH CRÈME FRAICHE

1 LARGE LEEK, GREEN LEAVES REMOVED
15ml EXTRA VIRGIN OLIVE OIL
455g ASPARAGUS SPEARS, WOODY ENDS REMOVED
560ml REDUCED SODIUM CHICKEN OR VEGETABLE BROTH, DIVIDED

220g SPRING PEAS (FRESH OR FROZEN)
225g LOW FAT PLAIN YOGURT
3 FRESH MINT LEAVES
125ml CRÈME FRAICHE FOR GARNISH (OPTIONAL)

Place the leek in the Single Serve Cup and pulse until chopped. Heat the oil on medium-high in a large saucepot and sauté the leek for 5 minutes. Add the asparagus spears and 235ml broth and bring to a boil. Reduce to a simmer, cover, and cook about 3 minutes. Add the peas. After another minute, remove from heat and let cool.

Working in batches, place the cooled mixture in the 1.1L Processing Bowl with the yogurt and mint leaves. Pulse until smooth. Pour into a serving bowl and add the remaining broth. Stir well and chill before serving. Garnish with a dollop of crème fraiche. Serves 4.

CAL 269, FAT 16G, SAT FAT 8G, CHOL 44MG, SODIUM 605MG,
CARBS 22G, PROTEIN 9G, FIBRE 6G, CALCIUM 165MG, POTASSIUM 587MG

anti-inflammatory

immune boost

mental boost

anti-aging skin, hair & eye health

detoxify & manage weight

digestion

ROASTED GARLIC & ROMA TOMATO SOUP

1kg FRESH ROMA TOMATOES,
SLICED IN HALF LENGTHWISE
1 MEDIUM YELLOW ONION, PEELED AND
CUT INTO QUARTERS
8 CLOVES GARLIC, PEELED
45ml EXTRA VIRGIN OLIVE OIL

3g SALT
PINCH GROUND BLACK PEPPER
250ml TOMATO JUICE
250ml HALF-AND-HALF CREAM
2g FRESH BASIL LEAVES, CHOPPED
30g HIGH-QUALITY CROUTONS FOR GARNISH

Preheat the oven to 190°C/Gas Mark 5. Place the tomatoes, onion, and garlic in a single layer on a baking pan. Avoid over-crowding the vegetables. Drizzle with the olive oil and season with salt and pepper. Roast for 45 minutes, turning once or twice. Remove from the oven and let cool.

Working in batches, place the roasted vegetables in the 1.1L Processing Bowl. Pulse each batch until smooth. Spoon into a large saucepan and add the tomato juice, cream and basil. Adjust the seasonings to taste. Warm over medium-low heat for about 5 minutes until barely simmering. Do not boil. Serve in 4 bowls with croutons to garnish. Serves 4.

CAL 286, FAT 20G, SAT FAT 7G, CHOL 24MG, SODIUM 513MG,
CARBS 25G, PROTEIN 6G, FIBRE 5G, CALCIUM 110MG, POTASSIUM 813MG

anti-inflammatory

immune boost

mental boost

relaxation & stress relief

anti-aging; skin, hair & eye health

detoxify & manage weight

digestion

energy boost

HEARTY VEGETABLE SOUP

1 MEDIUM YELLOW ONION, PEELED, ROUGHLY CUT

15ml EXTRA VIRGIN OLIVE OIL

130g KALE LEAVES

455g BROCCOLI FLORETS

750ml VEGETABLE BROTH

1 CARROT, PEELED AND SLICED

130g CORN KERNELS (CANNED OR FROZEN)

260g CANNED KIDNEY BEANS

115g COOKED PASTA SHELLS

6g SALT

PINCH CAYENNE PEPPER

1g GROUND BLACK PEPPER

GRATED PARMESAN CHEESE FOR GARNISH

Place the onion in the Single Serve Cup and pulse until evenly chopped. Sauté the onion in the oil in a saucepot on medium heat until soft. Add the kale leaves, broccoli and vegetable broth. Bring to a boil; then reduce to a simmer. Cover and simmer for 5 minutes. Remove from heat and let cool.

Working in batches, place the cooled mixture in the 1.1L Processing Bowl and pulse until smooth. Return to the saucepot. Add the carrots, corn, kidney beans and cooked pasta shells. Adjust the seasonings to taste and heat through on medium before serving. Garnish each serving with cheese. Makes 4 hearty servings.

CAL 213, FAT 6G, SAT FAT 2G, CHOL 5MG, SODIUM 1332MG,
CARBS 31G, PROTEIN 12G, FIBRE 5G, CALCIUM 151MG, POTASSIUM 602MG

SMOKED HAM, SWEET POTATO & APPLE SOUP

4 LARGE SWEET POTATOES, BAKED AND COOLED, SKINS REMOVED

510g NATURAL APPLESAUCE, DIVIDED

500ml REDUCED-SODIUM CHICKEN BROTH, DIVIDED

6g SALT (OR TO TASTE)

1g GROUND BLACK PEPPER

230g SMOKED HAM, CUT INTO BITE-SIZED CUBES

Place one-third each of the sweet potatoes, applesauce and chicken broth in the 1.1L Processing Bowl. Pulse each batch until smooth. Place the mixture in a large saucepot and bring the soup to a boil. Reduce to a simmer and season with salt and pepper to taste. Add the smoked ham and heat through again for a few minutes. Serves 4.

CAL 238, FAT 3G, SAT FAT 1G, CHOL 20MG, SODIUM 1525MG, CARBS 42G, PROTEIN 13G, FIBRE 5G, CALCIUM 62MG, POTASSIUM 719MG

anti-inflammatory

immune boost

relaxation & stress relief

anti-aging: skin, hair & eye health

detoxify & manage weight

energy boost

anti-inflammatory

mental boost

anti-aging: skin, hair & eye health

detoxify & manage weight

EAST INDIAN CURRIED
CAULIFLOWER SOUP

½ SMALL ONION, PEELED, ROUGHLY CUT

15ml EXTRA VIRGIN OLIVE OIL

2g CURRY POWDER

1g GROUND TURMERIC

PINCH GROUND SWEET PAPRIKA

6g SALT

1g GROUND BLACK PEPPER

450g CAULIFLOWER FLORETS

500ml VEGETABLE BROTH

Place the onion in the Single Serve Cup and pulse until chopped. Cook the onion in the oil in a saucepot over medium-high heat until soft. Add the curry powder, turmeric, sweet paprika, salt, and pepper and cook for an additional minute. Add the cauliflower and broth and bring to a boil. Reduce to a simmer, cover, and let cook about 10 minutes. Remove from heat and let cool.

Working in batches, place cooled soup in the 1.1L Processing Bowl and pulse until smooth. Season with additional salt and pepper as needed. Serve chilled or heat through and serve warm. Serves 3 to 4.

CAL 92, FAT 4G, SAT FAT 1G, CHOL 0MG, SODIUM 582MG,
CARBS 12G, PROTEIN 3G, FIBRE 5G, CALCIUM 38MG, POTASSIUM 488MG

anti-inflammatory

immune boost

mental boost

detoxify & manage weight

digestion

energy boost

SPEEDY CHICKEN TORTILLA SOUP

1 MEDIUM YELLOW ONION, PEELED, QUARTERED

1g CHILI POWDER

400g FIRE-ROASTED TOMATOES, WITH JUICE

1g FRESH CORIANDER

625ml CHICKEN BROTH

140g COOKED CHICKEN MEAT, SHREDDED

260g COOKED KIDNEY BEANS (USE CANNED, IF DESIRED)

SALT AND PEPPER TO TASTE

DICED AVOCADO, SOUR CREAM, AND TORTILLA STRIPS (OPTIONAL)

Place the onion, chili powder, tomatoes with juice and coriander in the 1.1L Processing Bowl and pulse until smooth.

Pour the tomato mixture into a saucepot and add the broth, chicken and kidney beans, stirring well to combine. Add salt and pepper to taste. Heat on medium, stirring often, until the soup is simmering. Serve with garnishes of diced avocado, sour cream, and tortilla strips, if desired. Serves 4.

**CAL 162, FAT 2G, SAT FAT 0G, CHOL 33MG, SODIUM 897MG,
CARBS 21G, PROTEIN 17G, FIBRE 5G, CALCIUM 68MG, POTASSIUM 592MG**

anti-inflammatory

immune boost

mental boost

relaxation &
stress relief

anti-aging: skin,
hair & eye health

detoxify &
manage weight

energy boost

BABY SPINACH SALAD
WITH CHAMPAGNE HONEY VINAIGRETTE

180g BABY SPINACH LEAVES

8 CREMINI MUSHROOMS, SLICED AND SAUTÉED

¼ SMALL RED ONION, PEELED, ROUGHLY CUT

30ml CHAMPAGNE VINEGAR

30ml EXTRA VIRGIN OLIVE OIL

40g RAW, UNFILTERED HONEY

6g SALT

1g GROUND BLACK PEPPER

60g CRUMBLED FETA CHEESE, FOR GARNISH

In a large mixing bowl, combine the spinach leaves and mushrooms. Set aside.

Place the red onion in the Single Serve Cup and pulse until chopped. Add the onion to the spinach and mushrooms. Place the vinegar, oil, honey, salt and pepper in the Single Serve Cup and pulse to blend. Drizzle the vinaigrette over the salad to taste. Garnish each serving with a sprinkling of feta cheese. Serves 4 to 6.

**CAL 138, FAT 9G, SAT FAT 3G, CHOL 9MG, SODIUM 724MG,
CARBS 9G, PROTEIN 4G, FIBRE 1G, CALCIUM 95MG, POTASSIUM 408MG**

CRISP BROCCOLI RABE
& BLACK OLIVE TAPENADE SALAD

1 CLOVE GARLIC, PEELED

225g BLACK OLIVES, PITTED

1 SMALL ROASTED PEPPER

5ml EXTRA VIRGIN OLIVE OIL

6g SEA SALT

5ml LEMON JUICE

8g FLAT LEAF PARSLEY

680g BROCCOLI RABE, STEAMED UNTIL CRISP, CHILLED

50g PARMESAN CHEESE, GRATED

Place all ingredients, except the broccoli rabe and cheese, into the 1.1L Processing Bowl and pulse, just until the olives are roughly chopped.

To assemble the salads, place the broccoli rabe equally on 4 plates and cover with a spoonful of the olive tapenade. Garnish each serving with the Parmesan cheese and serve right away. Serves 4.

CAL 245, FAT 16G, SAT FAT 3G, CHOL 11MG, SODIUM 1522MG,
CARBS 13G, PROTEIN 9G, FIBRE 3G, CALCIUM 289MG, POTASSIUM 19MG

anti-inflammatory

immune boost

mental boost

relaxation & stress relief

anti-aging skin, hair & eye health

detoxify & manage weight

digestion

anti-inflammatory

immune boost

mental boost

relaxation & stress relief

anti-aging: skin, hair & eye health

CHOPPED VEGETABLE SALAD
WITH DIJON VINAIGRETTE

140g CANNED SLICED BEETS, DRAINED

2 SPRING ONIONS, CUT IN HALF

4 SMALL FRESH CARROTS, PEELED, ROUGHLY CUT

215g SMALL BROCCOLI FLORETS

10g DIJON MUSTARD

15ml FRESH LEMON JUICE

30ml EXTRA VIRGIN OLIVE OIL

3g SALT

1g GROUND BLACK PEPPER

1g CAYENNE PEPPER

Place the beets, onions and carrots in the 1.1L Processing Bowl and pulse until largely chopped (do not over-mix). Spoon into a serving bowl and add the broccoli florets. Place the remaining ingredients in the Bowl and pulse until blended. Pour over the salad and toss well to combine. Serve right away or chill until serving. Serves 4.

**CAL 146, FAT 7G, SAT FAT 1G, CHOL 0MG, SODIUM 557MG,
CARBS 19G, PROTEIN 3G, FIBRE 5G, CALCIUM 56MG, POTASSIUM 470MG**

SUPER GREEN SUNFLOWER SALAD

½ BUNCH DARK GREEN KALE, RIBS REMOVED, TORN INTO BITE-SIZED PIECES

1 BUNCH SWISS CHARD, RIBS REMOVED, TORN INTO BITE-SIZED PIECES

½ SMALL RED ONION, PEELED, ROUGHLY CUT

½ CARROT, PEELED, ROUGHLY CUT

95g CANNED MANDARIN ORANGE SEGMENTS

15ml ORANGE JUICE

15ml RICE VINEGAR

5ml SESAME OIL

15ml TAMARI (OR SOY SAUCE/LOW-SODIUM SOY SAUCE)

2g SUGAR

35g SALTED SUNFLOWER SEEDS

Place the kale and Swiss chard in a large serving bowl. Place the onion and carrots in the 1.1L Processing Bowl and pulse to chop evenly. Spoon the vegetables over the greens and add the mandarin oranges.

Place the remaining ingredients, except the sunflower seeds, in the Bowl and pulse until blended. Pour over the salad, add the seeds, and toss well to combine. Chill before serving. Serves 4.

CAL 89, FAT 5G, SAT FAT 1G, CHOL 0MG, SODIUM 81MG,
CARBS 11G, PROTEIN 3G, FIBRE 11G, CALCIUM 73MG, POTASSIUM 388MG

anti-inflammatory

immune boost

mental boost

relaxation & stress relief

anti-aging, skin, hair & eye health

energy boost

anti-inflammatory

immune boost

mental boost

anti-aging; skin, hair & eye health

detoxify & manage weight

energy boost

BOK CHOY SALAD
WITH CASHEW DRESSING

285g RAW BOK CHOY, CHOPPED

2 FRESH CARROTS, PEELED, ROUGHLY CUT

2 STALKS CELERY, ROUGHLY CUT

3 SPRING ONIONS, CUT IN HALF

120g UNSALTED TOASTED CASHEWS,
   DIVIDED

15ml FRESH LEMON JUICE

5ml TAMARI (OR SOY SAUCE/LOW
   SODIUM SOY SAUCE)

45ml FLAXSEED OIL

3g SALT

1g GROUND BLACK PEPPER

Spoon the bok choy into a serving bowl. Place the carrots, celery and spring onions in the 1.1L Processing Bowl and pulse until finely chopped and add the mixture to the bok choy.

Place 60g cashews, lemon juice, tamari, flaxseed oil, salt and black pepper in the Bowl and pulse until blended. Pour the dressing over the salad and toss well to combine. Garnish each serving with the remaining toasted cashews. Serves 4.

CAL 221, FAT 19G, SAT FAT 3G, CHOL 0MG, SODIUM 455MG,
CARBS 11G, PROTEIN 5G, FIBRE 2G, CALCIUM 130MG, POTASSIUM 200MG

ORANGE FENNEL SALAD

2 LARGE FENNEL BULBS, FRONDS DISCARDED, SLICED

2 FRESH ORANGES, PEELED, SEGMENTED

½ SMALL RED ONION, PEELED, QUARTERED

4g FLAT LEAF PARSLEY

30ml FRESH ORANGE JUICE

15ml FRESH LEMON JUICE

45ml EXTRA VIRGIN OLIVE OIL

3g SALT

1g GROUND BLACK PEPPER

Place the fennel and orange segments in a large mixing bowl.

Place the onion, parsley, orange juice, lemon juice, olive oil, salt, and pepper in the Single Serve Cup and pulse until the onion is evenly chopped. Pour the dressing over the salad and toss well to combine. Serve right away or chill. Serves 4.

CAL 175, FAT 11G, SAT FAT 2G, CHOL 0MG, SODIUM 352MG,
CARBS 21G, PROTEIN 2G, FIBRE 6G, CALCIUM 91MG, POTASSIUM 672MG

anti-inflammatory

immune boost

mental boost

relaxation & stress relief

anti-aging, skin, hair & eye health

digestion

immune boost

mental boost

relaxation &
stress relief

digestion

energy boost

MEXICAN CHICKEN SALAD
WITH CHIPOTLE LIME DRESSING

140g COOKED CHICKEN, SHREDDED

250g COOKED BLACK BEANS

260g CORN KERNELS (FROZEN OR CANNED)

190g ROMAINE LETTUCE, SHREDDED

1 LARGE TOMATO, QUARTERED

1g FRESH CORIANDER

2 SPRING ONIONS, ROUGHLY CUT

1 CHIPOTLE PEPPER IN ADOBO SAUCE

120g LOW FAT PLAIN YOGURT

5ml FRESH LIME JUICE

3g SALT

PINCH GROUND BLACK PEPPER

Place the chicken, black beans, corn and lettuce in a large serving bowl.

Place the tomato, coriander and spring onions in the Single Serve Cup and pulse once or twice to evenly chop. Add the tomato mixture to the chicken and lettuce.

Place the pepper, yogurt, lime juice, salt and pepper in the Single Serve Cup and pulse until smooth. Pour the dressing over the salad and toss lightly. Serve at once. Serves 4.

CAL 189, FAT 2G, SAT FAT 1G, CHOL 32MG, SODIUM 583MG,
CARBS 25G, PROTEIN 17G, FIBRE 6G, CALCIUM 57MG, POTASSIUM 376MG

ASIAN SHRIMP SLAW
WITH GINGER SESAME VINAIGRETTE

420g NAPA (SAVOY) CABBAGE LEAVES,
    THINLY SLICED

1 LARGE RED PEPPER, SEEDED,
    QUARTERED

2g FRESH GINGER

145g SNOW PEAS, THINLY SLICED

450g COOKED LARGE SHRIMP,
    WITHOUT SHELLS

45ml RICE WINE VINEGAR

10ml SESAME OIL

5ml SOY SAUCE (OR LOW SODIUM
    SOY SAUCE)

30ml EXTRA VIRGIN OLIVE OIL

15g TOASTED SESAME SEEDS

SALT AND PEPPER TO TASTE

Place the cabbage in a serving bowl. Place the pepper and ginger in the Single Serve Cup and pulse to chop. Add to the cabbage. Add the snow peas and shrimp to the cabbage.

Place the rice wine vinegar, sesame oil, soy sauce and olive oil in the Single Serve Cup and pulse until blended. Pour the dressing over the salad and toss well to combine. Add salt and pepper to taste and serve right away. Top with the sesame seeds just before serving. Serves 4.

CAL 188, FAT 6G, SAT FAT 1G, CHOL 220MG, SODIUM 313MG,
CARBS 9G, PROTEIN 27G, FIBRE 3G, CALCIUM 125MG, POTASSIUM 558MG

anti-inflammatory

immune boost

mental boost

relaxation &
stress relief

anti-aging skin,
hair & eye health

detoxify &
manage weight

digestion

energy boost

anti-inflammatory

immune boost

mental boost

relaxation & stress relief

anti-aging; skin, hair & eye health

detoxify & manage weight

digestion

energy boost

BROCCOLI SALAD
WITH ALMOND MISO DRESSING

125g SILKEN TOFU

45g ALMOND BUTTER

30ml RAPESEED OIL

30ml WATER

30ml APPLE CIDER VINEGAR

40g SWEET WHITE MISO

12g SPRING ONION, CHOPPED

8g SUGAR

4g FRESH PARSLEY

10ml TAMARI (OR SOY SAUCE/LOW SODIUM SOY SAUCE)

2 HEADS BROCCOLI, CUT IN FLORETS, STEAMED AND CHILLED

Combine all ingredients, except the broccoli, in the Single Serve Cup and pulse until smooth. Pour the dressing over the broccoli to taste and toss well to combine. Serve right away. Serves 4. *(Cook's note: refrigerate remaining dressing in a tightly-covered container for up to 2 days.)*

CAL 256, FAT 17G, SAT FAT 2G, CHOL 0MG, SODIUM 610MG,
CARBS 22G, PROTEIN 11G, FIBRE 6G, CALCIUM 156MG, POTASSIUM 793MG

CHICKEN CAESAR SALAD

2 BONELESS, SKINLESS CHICKEN BREASTS, GRILLED AND SLICED

285g ROMAINE LETTUCE, TORN

125g SILKEN TOFU

60ml BUTTERMILK

30ml FRESH LEMON JUICE

15ml WHITE WINE VINEGAR

10g DIJON MUSTARD

1 CLOVE GARLIC, PEELED

2 CANNED ANCHOVIES

30g SEASONED SALAD CROUTONS

25g PARMESAN CHEESE, SHAVED

In a large mixing bowl, combine the chicken slices and the lettuce. Set aside.

In the Single Serve Cup, place the tofu, buttermilk, lemon juice, vinegar, mustard, garlic and anchovies. Pulse until creamy. Pour the dressing over the salad to taste and toss to coat. Add the croutons and Parmesan cheese just prior to serving. Serves 4 to 5.

**CAL 190, FAT 7G, SAT FAT 1G, CHOL 37MG, SODIUM 398MG,
CARBS 16G, PROTEIN 16G, FIBRE 2G, CALCIUM 105MG, POTASSIUM 282MG**

anti-inflammatory

mental boost

digestion

energy boost

anti-inflammatory

immune boost

mental boost

relaxation &
stress relief

anti-aging: skin,
hair & eye health

detoxify &
manage weight

digestion

energy boost

APPLE, RED ONION & CRANBERRY
SALAD WITH ALMOND VINAIGRETTE

180g BABY SPINACH LEAVES

1 LARGE RIPE GALA APPLE, PEELED, CORED AND SLICED

½ SMALL RED ONION, PEELED, THINLY SLICED

50g DRIED CRANBERRIES

60g CRUMBLED GOAT CHEESE

45ml SHERRY VINEGAR

60ml ALMOND OIL

3g DIJON MUSTARD

1g SALT

PINCH GROUND BLACK PEPPER

25g TOASTED, SLICED ALMONDS

In a large mixing bowl, combine the spinach, apple, onion, cranberries and cheese.

Combine the vinegar, oil, mustard, salt and pepper in the Single Serve Cup and pulse until blended. Toss the salad with the vinaigrette and top with the sliced almonds. Serves 4.

**CAL 384, FAT 20G, SAT FAT 4G, CHOL 11MG, SODIUM 257MG,
CARBS 25G, PROTEIN 7G, FIBRE 5G, CALCIUM 119MG, POTASSIUM 438MG**

THREE BEAN SALAD WITH
ITALIAN HERB VINAIGRETTE

2 STALKS CELERY, QUARTERED

½ SMALL RED ONION, PEELED, ROUGHLY CUT

30g FLAT-LEAF PARSLEY

2g FRESH BASIL

340g TRIMMED GREEN BEANS, CUT INTO 2.5cm PIECES, STEAMED AND COOLED

400g CHICKPEAS, DRAINED

400g RED KIDNEY BEANS, DRAINED

30ml EXTRA VIRGIN OLIVE OIL

30ml RED WINE VINEGAR

15ml LEMON JUICE

10g DIJON MUSTARD

6g SALT

1g GROUND BLACK PEPPER

Place the celery, onion, parsley and basil in the 1.1L Processing Bowl and pulse until chopped evenly.

Spoon the mixture into a large serving bowl and add the chickpeas.

Place the oil, vinegar, juice, mustard, salt and pepper in the Single Serve Cup. Pulse to blend and pour over the salad to taste. Toss well. Chill for at least 1 hour or up to overnight before serving. Serves 6.

**CAL 177, FAT 6G, SAT FAT 0G, CHOL 0MG, SODIUM 730MG,
CARBS 27G, PROTEIN 7G, FIBRE 7G, CALCIUM 63MG, POTASSIUM 383MG**

anti-inflammatory

immune booster

mental boost

anti-aging skin,
hair & eye health

detoxify &
manage weight

energy boost

immune boost

mental boost

anti-aging: skin, hair & eye health

energy boost

ROCKET, NECTARINE & PECAN
SALAD WITH BLUE CHEESE DRESSING

120-160g ROCKET LEAVES

2 RIPE NECTARINES, PITTED

30ml EXTRA VIRGIN OLIVE OIL

30ml FRESH LEMON JUICE

20g RAW, UNFILTERED HONEY

10g SHALLOT, PEELED, ROUGHLY CUT
   (OR USE SWEET WHITE ONION)

3g SALT

PINCH GROUND BLACK PEPPER

45g CRUMBLED BLUE CHEESE

35g TOASTED PECANS

Place the rocket on 4 individual salad plates. Set aside. Place the nectarines in the 1.1L Processing Bowl and pulse briefly to chop. Spoon the nectarines equally over the rocket.

Place the olive oil, lemon juice, honey, shallot, salt and pepper in the Bowl and pulse until smooth. Drizzle the dressing over each of the salads and top each salad with the blue cheese and toasted pecans. Serves 4.

CAL 255, FAT 20G, SAT FAT 5G, CHOL 8MG, SODIUM 454MG,
CARBS 15G, PROTEIN 5G, FIBRE 3G, CALCIUM 122MG, POTASSIUM 345MG

WHEATBERRY SALAD
WITH WALNUT SHALLOT VINAIGRETTE

½ SMALL RED ONION, PEELED, QUARTERED

30g FLAT-LEAF PARSELY

½ SMALL RED PEPPER, SEEDED,
QUARTERED

230g COOKED WHEATBERRIES, COOLED

45ml SHERRY VINEGAR

30ml WALNUT OIL

1 MEDIUM SHALLOT, PEELED (OR USE
SWEET WHITE ONION)

5g DIJON MUSTARD

3g SALT

PINCH GROUND BLACK PEPPER

60g WALNUTS, SHELLED

Place the onion, parsley and red pepper in the Single Serve Cup and pulse until chopped. Spoon the mixture into a large serving bowl and add the wheatberries. Mix to combine. Set aside.

Place the vinegar, oil, shallot, mustard, salt and pepper in the Single Serve Cup and pulse until blended. Pour the dressing over the salad and toss well. Chill at least 1 hour before serving. Just before serving, place the walnuts in the Single Serve Cup and pulse to chop. Mix the chopped walnuts into the salad and serve. Serves 3 to 4.

CAL 251, FAT 10G, SAT FAT 1G, CHOL 0MG, SODIUM 592MG,
CARBS 35G, PROTEIN 7G, FIBRE 0G, CALCIUM 13MG, POTASSIUM 109MG

anti-inflammatory

immune boost

relaxation &
stress relief

anti-aging: skin,
hair & eye health

BRUSSELS SPROUT SALAD
WITH MAPLE-MUSTARD DRESSING

175g WHOLE BRUSSELS SPROUTS, SLICED THINLY

100g CAULIFLOWER FLORETS, SLICED THINLY

170g CAN MANDARIN ORANGES, DRAINED

½ SMALL RED ONION, PEELED, ROUGHLY CUT

15ml DARK SESAME OIL

15ml RICE WINE VINEGAR

10ml PURE MAPLE SYRUP

10g DIJON MUSTARD

25g DRIED CRANBERRIES

Place the sprouts, cauliflower and mandarin oranges in a large serving bowl. Set aside. Place the red onion in the Single Serve Cup and pulse until chopped. Add the onion to the salad.

Place the sesame oil, vinegar, syrup and mustard in the Single Serve Cup and pulse to blend. Pour over the salad and add the cranberries. Toss well and serve at once. Serves 4.

**CAL 100, FAT 4G, SAT FAT 1G, CHOL 0MG, SODIUM 24MG,
CARBS 17G, PROTEIN 3G, FIBRE 4G, CALCIUM 36MG, POTASSIUM 319MG**

ALBACORE TUNA & DILL SALAD

2 STALKS CELERY, QUARTERED

¼ MEDIUM RED ONION, PEELED

4 SPEARS DILL PICKLE

510G CANNED ALBACORE TUNA,
   DRAINED AND CHUNKED

120g LOW FAT GREEK YOGURT

45g MAYONNAISE

3g FRESH DILL

10g DIJON MUSTARD

6g SALT

1g GROUND BLACK PEPPER

15ml CREAM (OR USE LOW FAT MILK),
   PLUS MORE TO TASTE

290g SALAD GREENS, RINSED AND KEPT CRISP

WHOLE GRAIN CRACKERS

Place the celery, onion and pickle in the 1.1L Processing Bowl and pulse to chop. Spoon the mixture into a large mixing bowl and add the tuna.

Place the yogurt, mayonnaise, dill, mustard, salt and pepper in the Single Serve Cup and pulse until smooth. Add cream as needed to taste. Pour the dressing over the tuna salad and mix well to coat. Serve on a bed of salad greens with whole grain crackers on the side. Serves 6 to 8.

CAL 85, FAT 3G, SAT FAT 0G, CHOL 13MG, SODIUM 461MG,
CARBS 5G, PROTEIN 7G, FIBRE 8G, CALCIUM 39MG, POTASSIUM 183MG

anti-inflammatory

immune boost

mental boost

relaxation &
stress relief

digestion

energy boost

CHAPTER SIX :: ENTRÉES & SIDE DISHES

BAJA FISH TACOS – P. 164

CHICKEN & JACK CHEESE ENCHILADAS – P. 157

TOMATOES GREMOLATA – P. 175

NEW ORLEANS CHICKEN & SHRIMP JAMBALAYA – P. 155

OLD EL PASO CHICKEN
WITH TOASTED PUMPKIN MOLE SAUCE

1 CUP HULLED PUMPKIN SEEDS, TOASTED

1 SMALL WHITE ONION, ROUGHLY CUT

3 CLOVES GARLIC, PEELED

4g FRESH CORIANDER, PLUS MORE FOR
   GARNISH

2 ROMAINE LETTUCE LEAVES, ROUGHLY TORN

½ FRESH CHILLI, SEEDED

1g GROUND CUMIN

625ml CHICKEN OR VEGETABLE BROTH,
   PLUS 250ml AS NEEDED

15ml RAPESEED OIL

6g SALT

4 SMALL BONELESS, SKINLESS CHICKEN BREASTS

780-1170g BROWN RICE, STEAMED AND KEPT WARM

 CORIANDER FOR GARNISH, OPTIONAL

Place the pumpkin seeds, onion, garlic, coriander, lettuce, fresh chilli and cumin in the 1.1L Processing Bowl. Add 115ml broth and pulse until smooth. Add 125ml broth and pulse again briefly. In a large skillet, heat the oil on medium-high heat. Add the blender mixture to the skillet and cook until very thick. Whisk in the remaining 375ml of chicken broth and add the salt and chicken. Add up to 250ml additional broth, if desired. Bring to a boil and reduce to a simmer; cook for 8 minutes or until chicken is cooked through and no pink remains. To serve, divide the rice between 4 dinner plates and top with the chicken and sauce. Garnish with coriander, if desired. Serves 4.

CAL 526, FAT 12G, SAT FAT 3G, CHOL 96MG, SODIUM 947MG,
CARBS 57G, PROTEIN 45G, FIBRE 4G, CALCIUM 63MG, POTASSIUM 687MG

anti-inflammatory

immune boost

relaxation &
stress relief

anti-aging: skin,
hair & eye health

digestion

energy boost

GUSTIAMO'S GRILLED PESTO CHICKEN

24g FRESH BASIL LEAVES

30ml EXTRA VIRGIN OLIVE OIL

35g TOASTED PINE NUTS

25g PARMESAN CHEESE, GRATED

30ml WATER

1 CLOVE GARLIC, PEELED

½ LEMON, JUICED

3g SALT

1g GROUND BLACK PEPPER

4 SMALL BONELESS, SKINLESS CHICKEN BREASTS, GRILLED OR BROILED

Place the basil, olive oil, pine nuts, cheese, water, garlic, lemon, salt and pepper in the 1.1L Processing Bowl. Pulse until smooth. To serve, place the cooked chicken breasts on 4 dinner plates and spoon the pesto sauce equally over each serving. Serves 4.

CAL 374, FAT 22G, SAT FAT 1G, CHOL 99MG, SODIUM 470MG, CARBS 2G, PROTEIN 38G, FIBRE 2G, CALCIUM 50MG, POTASSIUM 294MG

NEW ORLEANS CHICKEN
& SHRIMP JAMBALAYA

2 CLOVES GARLIC, PEELED

1 SMALL WHITE ONION, PEELED AND ROUGHLY CUT

45g GREEN PEPPER, SEEDED AND ROUGHLY CUT

180g CANNED FIRE-ROASTED DICED TOMATOES, WITH JUICES

4g CAJUN SEASONING

3ml TABASCO® SAUCE

500ml CHICKEN BROTH

185g LONG GRAIN WHITE RICE (OR QUICK-COOKING BROWN RICE)

225g COOKED CHICKEN THIGH MEAT, CUT INTO BITE-SIZED PIECES

225g MEDIUM SHRIMP, PEELED, DEVEINED

SALT AND PEPPER TO TASTE

Place the garlic, onion, peppers, tomatoes, seasoning and Tabasco® sauce in the 1.1L Processing Bowl and pulse just until chopped. Spoon into a large sauté pan and add the broth and rice. Bring to a boil on high heat; cover and reduce to a simmer for 20 minutes. Add the chicken and shrimp and cook for about 5 minutes until the shrimp are cooked through. Adjust seasonings to taste before serving. Serves 4.

CAL 320, FAT 11G, SAT FAT 3G, CHOL 81MG, SODIUM 567MG,
CARBS 30G, PROTEIN 11G, FIBRE 4G, CALCIUM 67MG, POTASSIUM 549MG

anti-inflammatory

immune booster

mental boost

relaxation & stress relief

detoxify & manage weight

digestion

energy boost

anti-inflammatory

immune boost

detoxify & manage weight

digestion

energy boost

SESAME CHICKEN LO MEIN

1 CLOVE GARLIC, CHOPPED

½ SMALL WHITE ONION, CHOPPED

30ml RAPESEED OIL, DIVIDED

1 RED PEPPER, SEEDED, CUT IN STRIPS

4 SMALL BONELESS, SKINLESS CHICKEN
   BREASTS, CUT IN STRIPS

5ml SESAME OIL

60ml TAMARI (OR USE LOW SODIUM SOY SAUCE)

30g CREAMY PEANUT BUTTER

PINCH GROUND BLACK PEPPER

225g SPAGHETTI NOODLES, COOKED,
   KEPT WARM

2g FRESH CORIANDER, CHOPPED

20g PEANUTS, CHOPPED

Sauté the garlic and onion in the rapeseed oil over medium-high heat. Add the peppers and chicken and reduce the heat to medium. Sauté for about 5 minutes, or until the chicken is no longer pink.

Meanwhile, pulse the sesame oil, tamari, peanut butter and black pepper in the Single Serve Cup until smooth. Stir into the chicken and peppers and heat through.

To serve, toss the chicken and peppers with the noodles and garnish with the coriander and peanuts before serving. Serves 4.

CAL 511, FAT 23G, SAT FAT 4G, CHOL 96MG, SODIUM 785MG,
CARBS 30G, PROTEIN 40G, FIBRE 3G, CALCIUM 30MG, POTASSIUM 428MG

anti-inflammatory

immune boost

mental boost

detoxify &
manage weight

digestion

energy boost

CHICKEN & JACK CHEESE ENCHILADAS

1 JALAPEÑO PEPPER, SEEDED AND ROASTED

795g CANNED WHOLE TOMATOES WITH JUICES

1 MEDIUM ONION, PEELED, ROUGHLY CUT

15ml RAPESEED OIL, PLUS MORE FOR TORTILLAS

500ml REDUCED-SODIUM CHICKEN BROTH

6g SALT

280g COOKED CHICKEN, SHREDDED

12 CORN TORTILLAS, WARMED

90g MONTEREY JACK CHEESE, SHREDDED

Place the pepper, tomatoes and onion in the 1.1L Processing Bowl and pulse until evenly chopped. Heat the oil in a large saucepan and add the chopped vegetables. Sauté until slightly thickened; add the chicken broth and salt. Reduce the heat and simmer the sauce for 10 minutes.

Preheat the oven to 180°C/Gas Mark 4. Spread 125ml of the sauce in a 23 x 33cm baking dish. Roll up a portion of the chicken in each tortilla, and place in the casserole dish, seam side down. Pour the remaining tomato sauce over the dish and top with the cheese. Bake until the enchiladas are heated through and the cheese is melted, about 20 minutes. Serves 4 to 6.

**CAL 275, FAT 10G, SAT FAT 5G, CHOL 40MG, SODIUM 743MG,
CARBS 29G, PROTEIN 18G, FIBRE 5G, CALCIUM 221MG, POTASSIUM 478MG**

anti-inflammatory

immune boost

mental boost

relaxation & stress relief

anti-aging, skin, hair & eye health

detoxify & manage weight

energy boost

GREEK CHICKEN WITH FETA
& OLIVE STUFFING

115g GREEK FETA CHEESE, CRUMBLED

285g FROZEN SPINACH, THAWED AND SQUEEZED DRY

8 KALAMATA OLIVES, PITTED

15ml EXTRA VIRGIN OLIVE OIL

15ml FRESH LEMON JUICE

4 BONELESS, SKINLESS CHICKEN BREASTS, SEASONED WITH SALT AND PEPPER

Preheat oven to 200°C/Gas Mark 6. Place the cheese, spinach, olives, oil and lemon juice in the 1.1L Processing Bowl. Pulse until the ingredients are mixed together and coarsely chopped. Set aside.

Make a horizontal slit in each chicken breast through the thickest part. Pack the stuffing into each breast, dividing the filling evenly. Use cooking string or a toothpick to secure the pocket, if needed.

Lightly coat a rimmed baking sheet with cooking spray and place the chicken breasts on the sheet. Bake for 8 minutes. Turn the chicken over and bake for another 8 minutes, or until cooked through and no pink remains. Remove string or toothpicks before serving. Serves 4.

**CAL 326, FAT 15G, SAT FAT 6G, CHOL 121MG, SODIUM 655MG,
CARBS 4G, PROTEIN 41G, FIBRE 1G, CALCIUM 198MG, POTASSIUM 307MG**

EASY TOMATO & BASIL CREAM SAUCE

1 RIPE ROMA TOMATO, SEEDED AND QUARTERED

35g TOMATO PUREE

125ml DOUBLE CREAM

6 BASIL LEAVES

1g DRIED ITALIAN SEASONING

Place all ingredients in the Single Serve Cup and pulse until smooth. Heat the sauce over medium heat in a small saucepan or heat briefly in the microwave.

Serve over hot, cooked pasta or add vegetables and/or cooked meat to create a complete entrée. Makes about 185g of sauce.

**CAL 81, FAT 8G, SAT FAT 5G, CHOL 27MG, SODIUM 35MG,
CARBS 4G, PROTEIN 1G, FIBRE 1G, CALCIUM 16MG, POTASSIUM 163MG**

anti-inflammatory

immune boost

mental boost

relaxation & stress relief

detoxify & manage weight

digestion

anti-inflammatory

mental boost

relaxation &
stress relief

anti-aging: skin,
hair & eye heath

detoxify &
manage weight

energy boost

GRILLED SALMON
WITH MAPLE DIJON SAUCE

30ml EXTRA VIRGIN OLIVE OIL

30g DIJON MUSTARD

15ml PURE MAPLE SYRUP

4g FRESH PARSLEY LEAVES

1 CLOVE GARLIC, PEELED

3g SALT

PINCH GROUND BLACK PEPPER

4 - 230g SALMON FILLETS, WITH SKIN

Preheat a grill to medium-high heat. In the Single Serve Cup, place the olive oil, mustard, syrup, parsley, garlic, salt and pepper. Pulse until smooth. Set aside one-half of the Dijon sauce. Brush the remaining half over the salmon fillets.

Grill the salmon over medium-high heat, 4 to 5 minutes on each side. Remove from grill and let rest for 5 minutes. Brush with the remaining sauce. Serves 4.

CAL 463, FAT 27G, SAT FAT 2G, CHOL 139MG, SODIUM 481MG,
CARBS 4G, PROTEIN 48G, FIBRE 0G, CALCIUM 36MG, POTASSIUM 22MG

ROASTED SALMON
WITH YOGURT DILL SAUCE

4 - 170g SALMON FILLETS, SEASONED WITH SALT, PEPPER AND BRUSHED WITH OLIVE OIL

200g LOW FAT PLAIN GREEK YOGURT

3g FRESH DILL

15ml FRESH LEMON JUICE

1 CLOVE GARLIC, PEELED

6g SALT

1g GROUND BLACK PEPPER

Preheat oven to 230°C/Gas Mark 8 degrees.

Lightly coat a baking dish with cooking spray and position the fillets in the dish. Roast in the oven for 10 minutes, until just cooked through.

Meanwhile, place the yogurt, dill, lemon juice, garlic, salt, and pepper in the Single Serve Cup and pulse until smooth. Serve each salmon fillet with a dollop of the dill sauce. Serves 4.

CAL 333, FAT 4G, SAT FAT 1G, CHOL 108MG, SODIUM 685MG,
CARBS 2G, PROTEIN 42G, FIBRE 0G, CALCIUM 67MG, POTASSIUM 581MG

anti-inflammatory

immune boost

mental boost

relaxation &
stress relief

anti-aging, skin,
hair & eye health

detoxify &
manage weight

energy boost

anti-inflammatory

immune boost

anti-aging: skin,
hair & eye health

detoxify &
manage weight

JAPANESE HALIBUT
WITH MISO-LIME GLAZE

40g WHITE MISO PASTE

30ml MIRIN OR SWEET WHITE WINE

15ml SOY SAUCE OR TAMARI (OR USE LOW SODIUM SOY SAUCE)

2g FRESH GINGER

15ml FRESH LIME JUICE

4 - 170g HALIBUT FILLETS (OR USE OTHER MILD, WHITE FISH FILLETS)

15g TOASTED SESAME SEEDS

Preheat oven to 230°C/Gas Mark 8.

Place the miso, mirin, soy sauce, ginger and lime juice in the Single Serve Cup and pulse until smooth. Brush the miso glaze mixture all over the halibut fillets.

Line a baking tray with foil and coat with cooking spray. Place the halibut on the tray and roast for 10 minutes, until just cooked through. Let rest 5 minutes and sprinkle with toasted sesame seeds. Serves 4.

**CAL 254, FAT 8G, SAT FAT 1G, CHOL55MG, SODIUM 693MG,
CARBS 5G, PROTEIN 39G, FIBRE 1G, CALCIUM 157MG, POTASSIUM 55MG**

GRILLED TILAPIA
WITH ROMESCO SAUCE

60ml EXTRA VIRGIN OLIVE OIL

1 SLICE CRUSTY BREAD, TORN AND TOASTED

50g BLANCHED, PEELED ALMONDS, TOASTED

5 CLOVES GARLIC, PEELED

425g CANNED WHOLE TOMATOES WITH JUICE

110g JARRED ROASTED RED PEPPERS,
  DRAINED

7g GROUND SMOKED PAPRIKA

30ml RED WINE VINEGAR

4 - 170g TILAPIA FILLETS, SEASONED WITH SALT
  AND PEPPER AND BRUSHED WITH OLIVE OIL
  (OR USE OTHER MILD, WHITE FISH FILLETS)

Preheat oven to 180°C/Gas Mark 4. Cover a rimmed baking sheet with foil. Set aside. Place the olive oil, bread, almonds, garlic, tomatoes, peppers, paprika and vinegar in the 1.1L Processing Bowl. Blend until smooth. Spread the mixture over the foil-covered baking sheet and bake in the oven for 15 minutes until the edges caramelize. Remove from heat and let cool.

Heat a grill to medium high heat. Grill the fish, 4-5 minutes per side. Remove and let rest for 5 minutes. Serve with the Romesco sauce drizzled on top. Serves 4.

**CAL 414, FAT 26G, SAT FAT 4G, CHOL 65MG, SODIUM 229MG,
CARBS 13G, PROTEIN 36G, FIBRE 0G, CALCIUM 103MG, POTASSIUM 927MG**

anti-inflammatory

immune booster

mental boost

relaxation &
stress relief

anti-aging: skin,
hair & eye health

detoxify &
manage weight

digestion

energy boost

anti-inflammatory

immune boost

relaxation &
stress relief

anti-aging: skin,
hair & eye health

digestion

energy boost

BAJA FISH TACOS

8g FRESH CORIANDER

1 LIME, JUICED

20g RAW, UNFILTERED HONEY

120g LOW FAT MAYONNAISE

¼ RED CABBAGE, THINLY SLICED

SALT AND BLACK PEPPER TO TASTE

45ml RAPESEED OIL

12 SMALL FRESH CORN TORTILLAS

**450g WHITE FISH FILLETS, CUT INTO
   BITE-SIZED PIECES**

1 AVOCADO, CHOPPED

130g CUP FRESH PREPARED SALSA

Place the coriander, lime juice, honey and mayonnaise in the 1.1L Processing Bowl and pulse until smooth. Place the cabbage in a large mixing bowl and spoon the dressing over, tossing lightly to mix. Season with the salt and pepper to taste. Chill.

In a large sauté pan, heat the oil until shimmering. Using tongs, quickly dip the tortillas into the oil just until the tortillas are softened. Drain the tortillas on paper towels. Remove all but 15ml of oil from the pan and heat on medium. Add the fish and sauté, stirring often, until slightly crispy and cooked through. Set aside and keep warm.

To assemble, place a spoonful of the cabbage slaw in one tortilla, top with a few pieces of fish and add the avocado and salsa. Repeat with the remaining tacos. Serve right away. Serves 4 to 6.

CAL 364, FAT 12G, SAT FAT 1G, CHOL 50MG, SODIUM 383MG,
CARBS 43G, PROTEIN 24G, FIBRE 8G, CALCIUM 64MG, POTASSIUM 379MG

GRILLED LAMB SKEWERS
WITH LEMON-GARLIC MINT SAUCE

4 CLOVES GARLIC, PEELED

30ml FRESH LEMON JUICE

60ml EXTRA VIRGIN OLIVE OIL

12g FRESH MINT LEAVES

680g TOP ROUND LAMB, CUT INTO
2.5cm CUBES

1 LARGE RED ONION, CUT INTO 2.5cm
SECTIONS

1 PINT CHERRY TOMATOES

6g SALT

1g GROUND BLACK PEPPER

WOODEN SKEWERS, SOAKED IN WATER

In the Single Serve Cup, place the garlic, lemon juice, olive oil and mint. Pulse until smooth. Reserve half of the mint sauce. Place the remaining half of the sauce in a medium mixing bowl with the lamb cubes. Cover and let marinate for 1 hour (or up to 8 hours).

Thread 3 to 4 lamb cubes on each wooden skewer, alternating with the red onion and cherry tomatoes. Season with the salt and pepper. Heat a grill to medium-high and grill the lamb skewers to medium-rare or medium for the lamb (about 6 to 10 minutes), turning 2-3 times. Place cooked skewers on a platter and drizzle with the reserved mint sauce. Serves 4.

CAL 377, FAT 10G, SAT FAT 6G, CHOL 107MG, SODIUM 676MG,
CARBS 5G, PROTEIN 34G, FIBRE 0G, CALCIUM 22MG, POTASSIUM 425MG

anti-inflammatory

immune boost

mental boost

anti-aging skin, hair & eye health

digestion

immune boost

mental boost

anti-aging: skin, hair & eye health

detoxify & manage weight

CRANBERRY-MUSTARD
ROASTED PORK LOIN

400g CANNED WHOLE CRANBERRY SAUCE

45g DIJON MUSTARD

1 SHALLOT, PEELED, ROUGHLY CUT (OR USE ¼ SMALL WHITE ONION)

15ml RED WINE VINEGAR

20g RAW, UNFILTERED HONEY

2g FRESH ROSEMARY LEAVES

1kg BONELESS PORK LOIN

SALT AND PEPPER TO TASTE

Preheat oven to 240°C/Gas Mark 9. Place the cranberry sauce, mustard, shallot, vinegar, honey, and rosemary in the 1.1L Processing Bowl. Pulse until smooth. Reserve half of the sauce.

Place the pork loin in a heavy roasting pan. Season with salt and pepper. Cover the loin with half of the sauce. Place in the oven and roast for 30-40 minutes, until internal temperature has reached 60°C. Remove from the oven and let rest 15 minutes. Serve with the reserved half of the cranberry sauce. Serves 6.

CAL 350, FAT 11G, SAT FAT 4G, CHOL 92MG, SODIUM 101MG,
CARBS 28G, PROTEIN 32G, FIBRE 1G, CALCIUM 20MG, POTASSIUM 480MG

BEEF FLANK STEAK
WITH CHIMICHURRI SAUCE

680g BEEF FLANK STEAK

SALT AND PEPPER FOR SEASONING

60g FRESH ITALIAN PARSLEY, PACKED

125ml EXTRA VIRGIN OLIVE OIL

80ml RED WINE VINEGAR

4g FRESH CORIANDER, PACKED

2 CLOVES GARLIC, PEELED

1g DRIED CRUSHED RED PEPPER

1g GROUND CUMIN

3g SALT

Preheat the oven to 230°C/Gas Mark 8. Place the steak in a roasting pan and season with salt and pepper. Roast for 15 minutes, reduce the heat to 180°C/Gas Mark 4 and roast for another 15 to 20 minutes, until the internal temperature of the meat reaches 52°C. Remove from the oven and let rest for 15 minutes. Slice thinly across the grain and keep warm.

Meanwhile, in the 1.1L Processing Bowl, pulse the remaining ingredients until smooth. To serve, fan the steak slices on a serving platter and drizzle with the Chimichurri Sauce. Serves 6.

CAL 188, FAT 16G, SAT FAT 5G, CHOL 60MG, SODIUM 231MG,
CARBS 2G, PROTEIN 23G, FIBRE 0G, CALCIUM 11MG, POTASSIUM 42MG

anti-inflammatory

immune boost

anti-aging, skin, hair & eye health

energy boost

anti-inflammatory

relaxation & stress relief

digestion

energy boost

CORNISH BEEF PASTIES

½ PÂTE BRISÉE (SEE P. 183)
4 SMALL POTATOES, PEELED, THINLY SLICED
½ WHITE ONION, PEELED, ROUGHLY CUT
8g FLAT LEAF PARSLEY
225g BEEF SIRLOIN STEAK, CUT IN LARGE PIECES
60g BUTTER
SALT AND PEPPER TO TASTE

Preheat the oven to 230°C/Gas Mark 8. Divide the dough into quarters and roll each into a 18cm circle. Place equal amounts of the potatoes in the center of each pastry circle.

Place the onion, parsley and beef in the 1.1L Processing Bowl and pulse until just chopped. Do not over-mix. Layer equally on top of the potatoes. Dot each pasty with the butter and generously salt and pepper to taste. To assemble, bring the edges of the pasty together, tucking in the ends, and crimp in a fluted pattern. Lightly pierce the pastry with a fork to allow the steam to escape. Place the pasties on a baking sheet and bake for 15 minutes. Reduce the heat to 180°C/Gas Mark 4 and continue baking for 30 minutes. Serve while warm. Serves 4.

CAL 435, FAT 13G, SAT FAT 7G, CHOL 11MG, SODIUM 587MG,
CARBS 26G, PROTEIN 25G, FIBRE 3G, CALCIUM 5MG, POTASSIUM 308MG

CHICKEN & GARDEN VEGGIE PASTIES

½ PÂTE BRISÉE (SEE P. 183)
4 SMALL POTATOES, PEELED, THINLY SLICED
½ WHITE ONION, PEELED, ROUGHLY CUT
1 LARGE CARROT, PEELED, CUT IN QUARTERS
110g PETITE POIS, FRESH OR FROZEN, THAWED
280g CHICKEN BREAST MEAT, COOKED, SHREDDED
4g FLAT-LEAF PARSLEY, CHOPPED
SALT AND PEPPER TO TASTE

Preheat the oven to 230°C/Gas Mark 8. Divide the dough into quarters and roll each into a 18cm circle. Place equal amounts of the potatoes in the center of each pastry circle.

Place the onion and carrot into the 1.1L Processing Bowl and pulse to chop. Remove and spoon on top of the potatoes. Layer the petite pois and chicken on each pasty. Scatter the parsley, salt and pepper over all. To assemble, bring the edges of the pasty together, tucking in the ends, and crimp in a fluted pattern. Lightly pierce the pastry with a fork to allow the steam to escape. Place the pasties on a baking sheet and bake for 15 minutes. Reduce the heat to 180°C/Gas Mark 4 and continue baking for 15 minutes. Serve while warm. Serves 4.

CAL 346, FAT 12G, SAT FAT 3G, CHOL 68MG, SODIUM 683MG,
CARBS 21G, PROTEIN 27G, FIBRE 3G, CALCIUM 44MG, POTASSIUM 569MG

immune boost

mental boost

relaxation & stress relief

anti-aging skin, hair & eye health

detoxify & manage weight

anti-inflammatory

immune boost

mental boost

relaxation &
stress relief

anti-aging: skin,
hair & eye health

detoxify &
manage weight

digestion

energy boost

TENDER-CRISP BROCCOLI
WITH FRESH HERB SAUCE

450g BROCCOLI FLORETS, STEAMED AND BLANCHED, WARM

60g WATERCRESS LEAVES, TIGHTLY PACKED

225g LOW FAT PLAIN YOGURT

60g LOW FAT MAYONNAISE

6g FRESH DILL

4g FRESH BASIL LEAVES

3g FRESH MINT LEAVES

1 SPRING ONION, ROUGHLY CUT

5ml RED WINE VINEGAR

3g SALT

Place the broccoli florets in a serving bowl.

Place the remaining ingredients in the 1.1L Processing Bowl and pulse until smooth. Pour over the broccoli florets and toss to coat. Serve while warm or chill before serving. Serves 4.

CAL 72, FAT 2G, SAT FAT 1G, CHOL 4MG, SODIUM 479MG,
CARBS 9G, PROTEIN 3G, FIBRE 0G, CALCIUM 116MG, POTASSIUM 155MG

SUGAR SNAP PEAS
WITH TAHINI MISO SAUCE

450g SUGAR SNAP PEAS, TRIMMED, STEAMED FOR 2 MINUTES AND BLANCHED

60ml WATER

20g LIGHT MISO

85g TAHINI (SESAME BUTTER)

1 CLOVE GARLIC, PEELED

2g LEMON ZEST

5ml FRESH LEMON JUICE

3g CHIVES

Place the sugar snap peas in a serving bowl and chill.

Place all remaining ingredients in the Single Serve Cup and pulse until smooth. Drizzle the sauce over the sugar snap peas and serve. Serves 4.

**CAL 158, FAT 12G, SAT FAT 2G, CHOL 2MG, SODIUM 196MG,
CARBS 5G, PROTEIN 2G, FIBRE 6G, CALCIUM 36MG, POTASSIUM 183MG**

anti-inflammatory

anti-aging; skin, hair & eye health

detoxify & manage weight

PARMESAN CAULIFLOWER CUPS

1kg CAULIFLOWER FLORETS, STEAMED UNTIL SOFT AND COOLED
115g LOW FAT SOUR CREAM
6g SALT
2g GROUND BLACK PEPPER
50g PARMESAN CHEESE, GRATED, PLUS MORE FOR TOPPING

Preheat the oven to 190°C/Gas Mark 5. Lightly coat 6 ramekins with cooking spray.

Place half each of the cauliflower, sour cream, salt, pepper and Parmesan cheese in the 1.1L Processing Bowl. Pulse briefly. Repeat with the remaining half of each ingredient. Portion out the mixture into the ramekins. Top with additional Parmesan cheese. Bake for 15 minutes, or until heated through and the cheese has become golden. Serves 6.

CAL 176, FAT 7G, SAT FAT 4G, CHOL 18MG, SODIUM 881MG,
CARBS 20G, PROTEIN 12G, FIBRE 7G, CALCIUM 162MG, POTASSIUM 887MG

SPRINGTIME PEA PUREE

285g FROZEN PEAS, COOKED, DRAINED

6g MINT LEAVES

60g LOW FAT SOUR CREAM

6g SALT

Place the peas in the 1.1L Processing Bowl. Pulse until evenly mixed. Add the remaining ingredients and pulse until smooth. Serve immediately or chill until serving. Serves 4.

CAL 88, FAT 3G, SAT FAT 2G, CHOL 10MG, SODIUM 23MG,

CARBS 9G, PROTEIN 4G, FIBRE 5G, CALCIUM 55MG, POTASSIUM 67MG

TENDER-CRISP ASPARAGUS
WITH HOLLANDAISE SAUCE

3 LARGE EGG YOLKS

30ml LEMON JUICE, DIVIDED

15ml WATER

5g DIJON MUSTARD

170g BUTTER, MELTED

3g FLAT LEAF PARSLEY

1g SALT

1g CAYENNE PEPPER

450g ASPARAGUS SPEARS, STEAMED
    TENDER-CRISP

Place the egg yolks, 15ml lemon juice, water and mustard in the 1.1L Processing Bowl. Pulse well to combine. Continue pulsing while pouring the melted butter in a very slow, steady stream through the pour spout, until the sauce has thickened. Add the parsley, salt, cayenne pepper and pulse for a few seconds. Add some of the remaining lemon juice to reach your desired consistency.

Drizzle the Hollandaise sauce over the steamed asparagus to serve. Serves 4. *(Cook's note: Store any remaining sauce in the refrigerator and use within 1 day.)*

CAL 246, FAT 25G, SAT FAT 15G, CHOL 166MG, SODIUM 151MG,
CARBS 3G, PROTEIN 3G, FIBRE 2G, CALCIUM 41MG, POTASSIUM 181MG

anti-inflammatory

immune boost

mental boost

detoxify &
manage weight

TOMATOES GREMOLATA

4 LARGE BEEFSTEAK TOMATOES, CORED, SEEDED AND CUT IN-HALF CROSSWISE

SALT AND PEPPER FOR SEASONING

5 SLICES STALE BREAD

3 SPRING ONIONS, ROUGHLY CUT

12 FRESH BASIL LEAVES

30g FLAT LEAF PARSLEY LEAVES

2 CLOVES GARLIC, PEELED

6g LEMON ZEST

EXTRA VIRGIN OLIVE OIL

30g GRUYERE CHEESE, GRATED

Preheat the oven to 200°C/Gas Mark 6. Place the tomatoes in a 23 x 33cm casserole dish and season with salt and pepper. Place the bread, onions, basil, parsley, garlic, and lemon zest in the 1.1L Processing Bowl and pulse until a bread crumb mixture is formed. Divide among the tomato halves, filling each tomato half compactly.

Drizzle each tomato with a little olive oil. Bake for 15 minutes. Top with the cheese and bake for an additional few minutes until the cheese has melted. Serves 4.

CAL 80, FAT 3G, SAT FAT 1G, CHOL 8MG, SODIUM 106MG,
CARBS 11G, PROTEIN 4G, FIBRE 2G, CALCIUM 86MG, POTASSIUM 308MG

CHAPTER SEVEN :: BREADS & BAKERY GOODS

HONEY CREPES – P. 195

QUEENSLAND BANANA BREAD – P. 185

FRESH PEAR GALETTE – P. 181

FRESH PEAR GALETTE

1 RECIPE PÂTE SUCRÉE (SEE FOLLOWING RECIPE)
60g APRICOT JAM
2 LARGE RIPE PEARS, THINLY SLICED
1 EGG, BEATEN
25g RAW SUGAR

Preheat the oven to 190°C/Gas Mark 5.

Roll the pastry dough on a floured board to form a 35.5cm round. Place the dough on a baking sheet. Brush the dough with the apricot jam and fan the pear slices into a circle, leaving a 5cm border. Fold the border up and around the pears, pressing gently. Brush the edge of the dough with egg and sprinkle with the raw sugar. Bake for 40 to 45 minutes until crust is golden and the pears are baked through. Let stand for 15 minutes before serving. Serves 4 to 6.

CAL 206, FAT 10G, SAT FAT 8G, CHOL 48MG, SODIUM 80MG,
CARBS 26G, PROTEIN 5G, FIBRE 11G, CALCIUM 15MG, POTASSIUM 86MG

anti-inflammatory

immune boost

mental boost

relaxation & stress relief

anti-aging, skin, hair & eye health

detoxify & manage weight

digestion

energy boost

mental boost

PÂTE SUCRÉE
(SWEET PASTRY DOUGH)

125 G UNBLEACHED, PLAIN FLOUR
12g SUGAR
1 EGG
PINCH SALT
90g COLD BUTTER, CUT INTO SMALL PIECES
60ml ICE WATER

Position the Dough Blade in the 1.1L Processing Bowl. Add the flour, sugar, egg, salt and butter and pulse just until combined. Add the ice water all at once and pulse again until the dough forms a rough ball. Remove and make a firm ball; flatten to a round disk shape. Chill until using. Makes 1 pastry crust.

digestion

CAL 148, FAT 17G, SAT FAT 6G, CHOL 25MG, SODIUM 71MG,
CARBS 13G, PROTEIN 3G, FIBRE 0G, CALCIUM 8MG, POTASSIUM 28MG

energy boost

mental boost

PÂTE BRISÉE
(BASIC PASTRY DOUGH)

135g VEGETABLE SHORTENING
6g SALT
80ml WATER, PLUS 15ml AS NEEDED
250g UNBLEACHED, PLAIN FLOUR

Position the Dough Blade in the 1.1L Processing Bowl. Add the shortening, salt and 80ml water and pulse briefly. Add the flour all at once and pulse again, scraping down the sides of the blender as needed. Add water as needed just until the dough begins to form.

Round the pastry into a ball and flatten to a round disk. Chill until ready to use. Makes 2 pastry crusts, serves 16. (Cook's note: this pastry is easy to roll and work with in pie and pastry recipes.)

digestion

CAL 133, FAT 9G, SAT FAT 3G, CHOL 18MG, SODIUM 15MG,
CARBS 12G, PROTEIN 2G, FIBRE 0G, CALCIUM 2MG, POTASSIUM 17MG

energy boost

anti-inflammatory

immune boost

mental boost

relaxation &
stress relief

anti-aging; skin,
hair & eye health

detoxify &
manage weight

digestion

energy boost

FRUIT CROSTADA

50g SUGAR

250g UNBLEACHED, PLAIN FLOUR

3g KOSHER SALT

225g COLD BUTTER, CUT INTO SMALL PIECES

60ml ICE WATER

330g FRESH FRUIT, ROUGHLY CUT

40g CASTOR SUGAR

Position the Dough Blade in the 1.1L Processing Bowl and add the sugar. Pulse for 30 seconds. Add the flour and salt and pulse again. Add the butter and pulse until the mixture resembles small peas.

Pour the ice water through the pour-spout and pulse quickly, just until the dough starts to form a mixture. Spoon out onto foil and quickly press together to form a rough disk. Cover and chill for 1 hour or in the freezer for 15-20 minutes.

Preheat the oven to 230°C/Gas Mark 8. Heavily flour a large piece of plastic wrap and quickly add the dough. Cover with another floured piece of wrap and roll to an 28cm circle. Remove the wrap pieces and place the dough on a cookie sheet. Toss the fruit gently with sugar and place in the center of the dough, leaving a 4cm border. Fold up and pleat around the outside edge to encase the fruit. Bake for 20-25 minutes, or until the dough is golden. Serves 6 to 8.

CAL 380, FAT 24G, SAT FAT 15G, CHOL 61MG, SODIUM 310MG,
CARBS 40G, PROTEIN 4G, FIBRE 1G, CALCIUM 18MG, POTASSIUM 104MG

QUEENSLAND BANANA BREAD

60g BUTTER

1 EGG

150g SUGAR

2 BANANAS, PEELED AND CUT IN HALF

45ml WHOLE MILK

2g BICARBONATE OF SODA

2g BAKING POWDER

250g UNBLEACHED, PLAIN FLOUR

65g MACADAMIA NUTS, CHOPPED

Preheat the oven to 180°C/Gas Mark 4. Position the Dough Blade into the 1.1L Processing Bowl. Add the butter, egg, sugar, bananas and milk to the Bowl and pulse until combined. Add the soda, powder, flour and macadamias and pulse again briefly. Scrape down the sides of the Bowl as needed.

Lightly coat a 23 x 13cm loaf pan with cooking spray and spoon the bread into the pan. Bake for 30 to 40 minutes, or until a toothpick comes out clean in the middle. Cool before slicing. Makes 1 loaf; 10 servings.

**CAL 266, FAT 11G, SAT FAT 4G, CHOL 31MG, SODIUM 49MG,
CARBS 51G, PROTEIN 4G, FIBRE 2G, CALCIUM 14MG, POTASSIUM 144MG**

mental boost

relaxation & stress relief

digestion

energy boost

anti-inflammatory

immune boost

mental boost

anti-aging: skin, hair & eye health

detoxify & manage weight

digestion

energy boost

DARK CHOCOLATE & CHERRY COOKIES

115g BUTTER

3 EGG WHITES

5ml VANILLA ESSENCE

140g DARK BROWN SUGAR

3g GROUND CINNAMON

125g WHOLE MEAL PASTRY FLOUR

160g OAT BRAN

4g BICARBONATE OF SODA

1g SALT

7g GROUND FLAXSEEDS

180g DARK SEMI-SWEET CHOCOLATE CHIPS

120g DRIED SWEET CHERRIES, ROUGHLY CHOPPED
   (**OR USE DRIED CRANBERRIES**)

Preheat oven to 180°C/Gas Mark 4. Place the Cookie Paddle in the 1.1L Processing Bowl and add the butter, egg whites and vanilla. Pulse until creamy. Add the sugar, cinnamon, flour, oat bran, soda, salt, and flaxseeds and pulse until just combined. Transfer to a mixing bowl and add the chocolate chips and cherries by hand. Cover and chill for 10 minutes.

Drop the dough by tablespoons onto nonstick cookie sheets, leaving 2.5cm between each cookie. Bake until golden, about 10 minutes. Makes 3 dozen.

CAL 200, FAT 6G, SAT FAT 3G, CHOL 7MG, SODIUM 137MG,
CARBS 38G, PROTEIN 4G, FIBRE 3G, CALCIUM 38MG, POTASSIUM 82MG

SWEET CARROT COOKIES

205g VEGETABLE SHORTENING

150g SUGAR

2 EGGS

130g CARROTS, PEELED, GRATED

250g UNBLEACHED, PLAIN FLOUR

10g BAKING POWDER

3g SALT

Preheat the oven to 190°C/Gas Mark 5.

Position the Cookie Paddle in the 1.1L Processing Bowl and add all ingredients. Pulse just until combined. Do not over-mix. Drop the batter by teaspoons onto a cookie sheet that has been lightly coated with cooking spray. Bake for 8 to 10 minutes. Makes about 3 dozen cookies; 2 cookies per serving.

CAL 196, FAT 12G, SAT FAT 5G, CHOL 27MG, SODIUM 118MG,
CARBS 20G, PROTEIN 7G, FIBRE 1G, CALCIUM 45MG, POTASSIUM 42MG

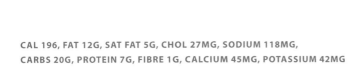

CANDIED GINGER COOKIES

190g UNBLEACHED, PLAIN FLOUR

125g WHOLE WHEAT PASTRY FLOUR

4g GROUND GINGER

3g GROUND CINNAMON

1g GROUND CLOVES

1g SALT

170g BUTTER

250g RAW, UNFILTERED HONEY

1 EGG

15ml BLACKSTRAP MOLASSES

10g CANDIED GINGER, FINELY CHOPPED

Preheat the oven to 180°C/Gas Mark 4.

Whisk the flours, ginger, cinnamon, cloves and salt until combined. Set aside. Place the Cookie Paddle in the 1.1L Processing Bowl and pulse the butter, honey, egg and molasses until well-combined. Add the dry ingredients and the ginger and pulse just until mixed.

Chill dough for 10 minutes. Drop the dough by teaspoonsful on nonstick cookie sheets about 2.5cm apart. Bake for 8 to 10 minutes and cool on wire racks before serving. Makes 3 dozen; 2 per serving.

CAL 132, FAT 8G, SAT FAT 4G, CHOL 12MG, SODIUM 172MG,
CARBS 29G, PROTEIN 5G, FIBRE 1G, CALCIUM 22MG, POTASSIUM 67MG

SLICE & BAKE BUTTERY
LEMON COOKIES

225g BUTTER

100g RAW SUGAR

PINCH SALT

1 LARGE EGG

5ml LEMON ESSENCE

125g WHOLE WHEAT PASTRY FLOUR

190g UNBLEACHED PLAIN FLOUR

Position the Cookie Paddle in the 1.1L Processing Bowl and place the butter and sugar inside. Pulse until fluffy. Add the salt, egg and lemon essence and blend until smooth. Add the flours and pulse until just combined. Remove dough from the Bowl and roll into two logs. Wrap each log in plastic wrap and place in the refrigerator to chill for at least 1 hour.

Preheat the oven to 200°C/Gas Mark 6. Remove dough from the plastic wrap and cut to form 5mm thick slices. Place onto nonstick cookie sheets and bake for 8 to 10 minutes until slightly golden brown. Cool on wire racks before serving. Makes about 3 dozen; 1 cookie per serving.

CAL 194, FAT 11G, SAT FAT 7G, CHOL 37MG, SODIUM 91MG,
CARBS 17G, PROTEIN 2G, FIBRE 0G, CALCIUM 11MG, POTASSIUM 39MG

mental boost

detoxify &
manage weight

digestion

energy boost

anti-inflammatory

immune boost

mental boost

relaxation &
stress relief

anti-aging: skin,
hair & eye health

detoxify &
manage weight

digestion

energy boost

FIG & ALMOND GRANOLA BARS

160g ROLLED OATS

70g SHELLED, UNSALTED RAW SUNFLOWER SEEDS

60g TOASTED WHEAT GERM

30g WHOLE WHEAT PASTRY FLOUR

75g DRIED FIGS, ROUGHLY CHOPPED (OR USE ANY DRIED FRUIT)

70g RAW ALMONDS

60g NONFAT DRY MILK

3g GROUND CINNAMON

85g RAW, UNFILTERED HONEY

60ml PURE MAPLE SYRUP

2 LARGE EGGS

Preheat oven to 180°C/Gas Mark 4. Coat a 23cm x 23cm baking pan with cooking spray. Set aside.

Place the oats, sunflower seeds, wheat germ, flour, figs, almonds, dried milk, and cinnamon into the 1.1L Processing Bowl and pulse 5 or 6 times. Add the honey, syrup, and eggs and pulse until combined. Place the dough into the baking pan and use a spatula to evenly spread. Bake for 20 minutes, until lightly browned. Allow to cool for 15 minutes before slicing into bars. Makes about 27 bars; 2 bars per serving.

**CAL 133, FAT 5G, SAT FAT 1G, CHOL 21MG, SODIUM 19MG,
CARBS 19G, PROTEIN 4G, FIBRE 2G, CALCIUM 54MG, POTASSIUM 158MG**

ALMOND MACAROONS

125ml ORANGE JUICE

190g BLANCHED ALMONDS, DIVIDED

400g SUGAR, DIVIDED

6 EGG WHITES, DIVIDED

30g CAKE FLOUR, DIVIDED

1g SALT, DIVIDED

80g ICING SUGAR

Preheat oven to 150°C/Gas Mark 2. Place the orange juice, 85g almonds and 200g sugar in the 1.1L Processing Bowl. Pulse for 1 minute until very fine. Add the remaining almonds and pulse for another 30 seconds. Transfer one-half of the dough to a self-sealing plastic bag and chill.

Add half of the remaining ingredients to the dough in the Bowl and pulse until incorporated. Drop by teaspoons onto parchment-covered baking sheets. Let stand 30 minutes, then bake for 25 minutes. Repeat with the remaining almond paste and cookie ingredients. Cool completely before serving. Makes about 3 dozen cookies; 2 cookies per serving.

CAL 208, FAT 8G, SAT FAT 1G, CHOL 0MG, SODIUM 51MG,
CARBS 33G, PROTEIN 5G, FIBRE 2G, CALCIUM 42MG, POTASSIUM 151MG

anti-inflammatory

immune boost

mental boost

relaxation & stress relief

anti-aging skin, hair & eye health

detoxify & manage weight

energy boost

WALNUT & RAISIN
CINNAMON ROLLS

1 PKG ACTIVE "QUICK RISE" DRY YEAST	410g UNBLEACHED, PLAIN FLOUR
50g RAW SUGAR	140g BROWN SUGAR
3g SALT	8g GROUND CINNAMON
60ml WARM WATER (43-46°C)	115g BUTTER, SOFTENED
180ml WARM WHOLE MILK	30g TOASTED WALNUTS, CHOPPED
60g BUTTER, MELTED	35g RAISINS
1 EGG	

Position the Dough Blade in the 1.1L Processing Bowl. Add the yeast, sugar, salt, water, milk, butter and egg and pulse 2 to 3 times. Mix in the flour 30g at a time, pulsing after each addition. Pulse off and on for 2 minutes, adding more flour if needed to form a soft dough. Place dough in a greased bowl, cover and let rise for 1 hour. Meanwhile, combine the brown sugar, cinnamon, and butter in a medium bowl.

Preheat the oven to 180°C/Gas Mark 4. Roll the dough into a large rectangle and spread with the cinnamon mixture. Sprinkle with walnuts and raisins. Roll up the dough like a jelly roll. Pinch seam and ends. Cut into 12 rolls. Place in a greased 23 x 33cm pan. Cover and let rise an additional 45 minutes. Bake for 25 minutes or until golden. Makes 12 rolls.

CAL 343, FAT 14G, SAT FAT 7G, CHOL 48MG, SODIUM 200MG,
CARBS 50G, PROTEIN 5G, FIBRE 1G, CALCIUM 50MG, POTASSIUM 173MG

anti-inflammatory

immune boost

anti-aging, skin,
hair & eye health

digestion

RAISIN MOLASSES MUFFINS

125g WHOLE MEAL FLOUR

90g WHEAT BRAN

3g SALT

5g BICARBONATE OF SODA

2 LARGE EGGS

350ml LOW FAT BUTTERMILK

45ml RAPESEED OIL

15ml BLACKSTRAP MOLASSES

70g DARK BROWN SUGAR

70g RAISINS

Preheat oven to 200°C/Gas Mark 6. Position the Dough Blade in the 1.1L Processing Bowl. Add the flour, bran, salt and soda and pulse 1 or 2 times. Add the eggs, buttermilk, oil, molasses and sugar and pulse again just until combined. Add the raisins by hand and spoon into prepared muffin tins. Bake for 15-20 minutes. Makes 12 muffins.

**CAL 180, FAT 8G, SAT FAT 5G, CHOL 36MG, SODIUM 144MG,
CARBS 27G, PROTEIN 2G, FIBRE 1G, CALCIUM 47MG, POTASSIUM 119MG**

anti-inflammatory

immune boost

mental boost

relaxation & stress relief

anti-aging: skin, hair & eye health

detoxify & manage weight

digestion

energy boost

BLUEBERRY LEMON MUFFINS

125g WHOLE MEAL FLOUR

210g UNBLEACHED, PLAIN FLOUR

14g BICARBONATE OF SODA

170g RAW, UNFILTERED HONEY

2 EGGS

180ml WHOLE MILK

150g BUTTER, MELTED

225g FRESH BLUEBERRIES

6g LEMON ZEST

Preheat oven to 200°C/Gas Mark 6.

Position the Dough Blade in the 1.1L Processing Bowl. Place the flours and soda in the Bowl and add the honey, eggs, milk and melted butter. Pulse just until combined. Fold in the blueberries and lemon zest with a spoon and pour into prepared muffin tins. Bake for 18-20 minutes. Makes 12 muffins.

CAL 263, FAT 12G, SAT FAT 7G, CHOL 57MG, SODIUM 196MG,
CARBS 36G, PROTEIN 5G, FIBRE 1G, CALCIUM 3MG, POTASSIUM 87MG

HONEY CREPES

2 LARGE EGGS

180ml WHOLE MILK

125ml WATER

125g UNBLEACHED, PLAIN FLOUR

45g BUTTER, MELTED

5ml VANILLA ESSENCE

20g RAW, UNFILTERED HONEY

OIL AS NEEDED

HONEY FOR DRIZZLING

ICING SUGAR

Place the Dough Blade in the 1.1L Processing Bowl. Add the eggs, milk, water, flour, butter, essence and 20g honey and pulse until smooth.

In a nonstick sauté pan, heat a little oil over medium-high heat. Pour a small amount of batter into the pan and swirl around evenly to form a thin circle. Cook for 30 seconds. Flip and cook for an additional 10 seconds. Remove and keep warm on a plate.

Continue with the remaining batter, stacking the crepes between layers of parchment paper. To serve, roll the crepes to form cigar shapes, place on a serving platter, and drizzle with honey. Sift with icing sugar just before serving. Makes 4 servings; 2 crepes per serving.

CAL 272, FAT 12G, SAT FAT 6G, CHOL 118MG, SODIUM 145MG,
CARBS 29G, PROTEIN 10G, FIBRE 1G, CALCIUM 126MG, POTASSIUM 218MG

mental boost

detoxify &
manage weight

digestion

energy boost

anti-inflammatory

WHOLE MEAL PIZZA/FLATBREAD DOUGH

7g PKG DRY ACTIVE YEAST

6g SALT

12g SUGAR

160ml WARM WATER (43°-46°C)

60ml EXTRA VIRGIN OLIVE OIL

125g UNBLEACHED, PLAIN FLOUR

160g WHOLE MEAL FLOUR

Position the Dough Blade in the 1.1L Processing Bowl. Place the yeast, salt, sugar and water inside and pulse briefly. Add the oil and flours, 60g at a time, pulsing 3 times between each addition. Pulse until a ball forms. Transfer dough to a lightly-oiled bowl and cover. Let rise for about an hour. Makes 1 pizza or flatbread.

(Cook's note: you can store this dough in the refrigerator, in a self-sealing plastic bag with a little olive oil, for up to one week.)

digestion

energy boost

CAL 240, FAT 12G, SAT FAT 2G, CHOL 0MG, SODIUM 581MG,
CARBS 28G, PROTEIN 4G, FIBRE 1G, CALCIUM 5MG, POTASSIUM 34MG

ITALIAN BREADSTICKS

1 WHOLE MEAL PIZZA DOUGH (SEE PRECEDING RECIPE)
30ml EXTRA VIRGIN OLIVE OIL
1g DRIED OREGANO
1g DRIED ROSEMARY
25g PARMESAN CHEESE, GRATED

Preheat the oven to 190°C/Gas Mark 5.

Roll the dough into a 15 x 20cm rectangle. Cut the dough into 2cm strips. Twist each strip and place on a greased baking sheet. Cover and let rise in a warm place for 1 hour. Brush with oil and sprinkle with the oregano, rosemary, and cheese. Bake for 12 to 15 minutes until golden brown. Makes 10 to 12 breadsticks.

CAL 284, FAT 16G, SAT FAT 3G, CHOL 0MG, SODIUM 623MG,
CARBS 28G, PROTEIN 4G, FIBRE 1G, CALCIUM 40MG, POTASSIUM 38MG

anti-inflammatory

immune boost

mental boost

digestion

energy boost

anti-inflammatory

immune boost

mental boost

anti-aging: skin, hair & eye health

detoxify & manage weight

digestion

SUMMER VEGETABLE FLATBREAD

1 SMALL COURGETTE, SLICED INTO 5mm THICK ROUNDS

1 SMALL RED PEPPER, SLICED INTO 5mm WIDE STRIPS

1 SMALL AUBERGINE, SLICED INTO 5mm THICK ROUNDS

30ml EXTRA VIRGIN OLIVE OIL

SALT AND PEPPER TO TASTE

1 WHOLE MEAL PIZZA DOUGH (SEE P. 196)

65g FONTINA CHEESE, SHREDDED

25g PARMESAN CHEESE, GRATED

CORNMEAL FOR DUSTING

Preheat the broiler to High. In a large mixing bowl, combine the courgette, pepper and aubergine and toss with the olive oil, salt and pepper. Place the vegetables in a single layer on a baking sheet and broil for 8 minutes, turning once halfway through.

Heat the oven to 230°C/Gas Mark 8. Sprinkle a 26cm x 38cm baking sheet with cornmeal and roll out or press the dough by hand on the sheet. It should be very thin. Top with the broiled vegetables and scatter the cheeses over the top. Bake for 10 to 15 minutes, until cheeses are melted and crust is golden brown. (For a crisper crust, use a pizza stone for baking.) Serves 4 to 6.

CAL 412, FAT 25G, SAT FAT 7G, CHOL 20MG, SODIUM 772MG,
CARBS 38G, PROTEIN 10G, FIBRE 6G, CALCIUM 152MG, POTASSIUM 442MG

anti-inflammatory

relaxation & stress relief

detoxify & manage weight

digestion

energy boost

APPLE, PROSCUITTO, & CARAMELIZED ONION FLATBREAD

1 WHOLE MEAL PIZZA DOUGH (SEE P. 196)

125ml CRÈME FRAICHE

1 LARGE YELLOW ONION, THINLY SLICED AND CARAMELIZED IN A SAUTÉ PAN

4 SLICES PROSCUITTO, BROWNED AND CRUMBLED (OR USE BACON)

½ SMALL FUJI APPLE, THINLY SLICED

60g ROMANO CHEESE, GRATED

8g FLAT-LEAF PARSLEY

CORNMEAL FOR DUSTING

Preheat the oven to 230°C/Gas Mark 8.

Sprinkle a 26cm x 40cm baking tray with cornmeal and roll out or press the dough by hand on the sheet. It should be very thin. Spread a thin layer of crème fraiche over the flatbread and layer with the onions, proscuitto, apple slices, and cheese. Scatter the parsley over all and bake for 10 to 15 minutes, until the cheese has melted and the crust is golden brown. (For a crisper crust, use a pizza stone for baking.) Serves 4 to 6.

CAL 383, FAT 25G, SAT FAT 12G, CHOL 57MG, SODIUM 615MG,
CARBS 25G, PROTEIN 13G, FIBRE 2G, CALCIUM 250MG, POTASSIUM 98MG

anti-inflammatory

immune boost

mental boost

relaxation & stress relief

detoxify & manage weight

energy boost

MARGHERITA FLATBREAD

1 WHOLE MEAL PIZZA DOUGH (SEE P. 196)
45g TOMATO SAUCE
1 MEDIUM BEEFSTEAK TOMATO, THINLY SLICED
115g FRESH MOZZARELLA BALL, THINLY SLICED
10 FRESH BASIL LEAVES, DIVIDED
EXTRA VIRGIN OLIVE OIL
CORNMEAL FOR DUSTING

Preheat the oven to 230°C/Gas Mark 8.

Sprinkle a 26cm x 40cm baking sheet with cornmeal and roll out or press the dough by hand on the sheet. It should be very thin. Brush with the tomato sauce. Top with the tomato slices, mozzarella slices, and half of the basil leaves. Bake for 10 to 15 minutes, until the cheese has melted and the crust is golden brown. Top with the remaining basil leaves and a drizzle of olive oil before serving. Serves 4.

CAL 348, FAT 22G, SAT FAT 5G, CHOL 10MG, SODIUM 621MG,
CARBS 30G, PROTEIN 8G, FIBRE 2G, CALCIUM 109MG, POTASSIUM 132MG

WARM TOMATO & MOZZARELLA TART

125g UNBLEACHED PLAIN FLOUR

1g SALT

90g COLD BUTTER, CUT IN SMALL PIECES

60ml COLD WATER

60ml MOZZARELLA CHEESE, SHREDDED

1 SMALL ONION, PEELED AND SLICED

2 ROMA TOMATOES, SLICED

COARSE SEA SALT

GROUND BLACK PEPPER

4g FRESH BASIL

Preheat the oven to 200°C/Gas Mark 6.

Position the Dough Blade in the 1.1L Processing Bowl and add the flour, salt and butter. Pulse until crumbly. Add the water and pulse again until the pastry forms into a rough ball. Form into a flattened disk.

Roll the pastry dough to a 36cm circle and fit into a 25.5cm tart pan (or use a pie pan), trimming the edges.

Layer the cheese, onion and tomatoes over the pastry and sprinkle with the salt and pepper. Scatter the basil over all. Bake for 30 to 35 minutes. Cut into wedges and serve while warm. Serves 4 to 6.

CAL 237, FAT 15G, SAT FAT 9G, CHOL 43MG, SODIUM 420MG,
CARBS 19G, PROTEIN 7G, FIBRE 1G, CALCIUM 161MG, POTASSIUM 116MG

anti-inflammatory

immune boost

mental boost

relaxation &
stress relief

detoxify &
manage weight

CHAPTER EIGHT :: DELECTABLE DESSERTS

FRESH MANGO FOOL – P. 218

ITALIAN TIRAMISU PARFAITS – P. 207

BERRY BERRY CRISP – P. 214

anti-inflammatory

mental boost

anti-aging, skin, hair & eye health

ITALIAN TIRAMISU PARFAITS

250g MASCARPONE CHEESE

25g SUGAR

30ml BRANDY

1 PKG SPONGEFINGERS

375ml STRONG COFFEE

60g WHIPPED CREAM

TOASTED ALMONDS

SHAVED CHOCOLATE

Position the Dough Blade in the 1.1L Processing Bowl. Place the cheese, sugar and brandy in the Bowl and pulse until smooth.

To assemble 4 parfaits, spoon a small amount of the cheese mixture in each of 4 wide glasses. Dip 2 spongefingers into the coffee and place on top of the cheese. Repeat with another layer of cheese to each parfait and repeat with the spongefingers. Repeat the layers until the ingredients are used. Add a dollop of whipped cream to each parfait. Finish each with toasted almonds and shaved chocolate. Serve at once. Serves 4.

**CAL 249, FAT 19G, SAT FAT 11G, CHOL 57MG, SODIUM 26MG,
CARBS 12G, PROTEIN 3G, FIBRE 0G, CALCIUM 10MG, POTASSIUM 11MG**

anti-inflammatory

immune boost

mental boost

relaxation &
stress relief

anti-aging: skin,
hair & eye health

detoxify &
manage weight

energy boost

SILKY LEMON CREAM
WITH BLUEBERRIES

125g LOW FAT CREAM CHEESE

150g PLAIN GREEK YOGURT

2ml LEMON ESSENCE

40g RAW, UNFILTERED HONEY

300g FRESH BLUEBERRIES, RINSED

Place the cream cheese, yogurt, lemon essence and honey in the 1.1L Processing Bowl. Pulse until whipped and smooth.

Layer the lemon cream and blueberries in dessert dishes or wineglasses. Chill or serve at once. Serves 4.

**CAL 164, FAT 7G, SAT FAT 4G, CHOL 18MG, SODIUM 106MG,
CARBS 23G, PROTEIN 9G, FIBRE 2G, CALCIUM 89MG, POTASSIUM 113MG**

ALMOND SHORTCRUST

25g BLANCHED, WHOLE ALMONDS

220g PLAIN FLOUR

40g ICING SUGAR

90g BUTTER, SOFTENED

PINCH KOSHER SALT

1 VANILLA BEAN, SEEDED, POD DISCARDED

2 EGG YOLKS

Place the almonds in the 1.1L Processing Bowl. Process the nuts until finely ground. Add the remaining ingredients and pulse until the dough forms a ball. Cover and chill for 30 minutes.

Preheat the oven to 180°C/Gas Mark 4. To prepare a tart pastry, roll out the dough between two sheets of plastic wrap and fit into a tart pan. Place the pan on a cookie sheet and bake for 20 minutes. Fill as your recipe directs. Makes 1 large or 2 medium tart shells.

CAL 186, FAT 10G, SAT FAT 5G, CHOL 60MG, SODIUM 67MG,
CARBS 22G, PROTEIN 4G, FIBRE 1G, CALCIUM 17MG, POTASSIUM 50MG

mental boost

anti-aging skin, hair & eye health

detoxify & manage weight

energy boost

anti-inflammatory
immune boost
mental boost
relaxation & stress relief
anti-aging: skin, hair & eye heath
detoxify & manage weight
digestion
energy boost

FRESH FRUIT & LEMON
CREAM TART

500g LOW FAT CREAM CHEESE (OR USE NEUCHATEL CHEESE), SOFTENED

65g SUGAR

1 LEMON, JUICED

1 RECIPE ALMOND SHORTCRUST DOUGH, BAKED AND COOLED (SEE P. 209)

825g FRESH FRUIT, SUCH AS BERRIES, KIWI OR STONE FRUIT (SLICED)

225g CURRANT JELLY, MELTED (OR USE OTHER FRUIT JELLY)

Position the Dough Paddle in the 1.1L Processing Bowl and add the cream cheese, sugar and lemon juice. Pulse until smooth.

Spoon the cream cheese mixture evenly onto the cooled pastry and smooth the top with a knife. Arrange the fruit in concentric circles over the cheese mixture and brush with the melted jelly. Chill to set. Serves 10.

**CAL 406, FAT 18G, SAT FAT 10G, CHOL 85MG, SODIUM 210MG,
CARBS 55G, PROTEIN 10G, FIBRE 2G, CALCIUM 73MG, POTASSIUM 305MG**

STRAWBERRY BASIL ICE CREAM

300g STRAWBERRIES, STEMMED AND HULLED
200g SUGAR
15 FRESH BASIL LEAVES
500ml WHOLE MILK
500ml LIGHT CREAM
10ml VANILLA ESSENCE

Place the strawberries, sugar and basil in the 1.1L Processing Bowl. Pulse until the strawberry mixture is smooth. Spoon into a large bowl, add the remaining ingredients and stir to combine.

Pour the ice cream mixture into the freezer bowl or tub of your ice cream maker and proceed as directed. Makes 950g.

CAL 225, FAT 9G, SAT FAT 6G, CHOL 29MG, SODIUM 50MG,
CARBS 34G, PROTEIN 4G, FIBRE 1G, CALCIUM 140MG, POTASSIUM 223MG

anti-inflammatory

immune boost

mental boost

anti-aging; skin, hair & eye health

detoxify & manage weight

energy boost

immune boost

anti-aging: skin, hair & eye health

CREAMY DREAMY CHEESECAKE

10 DIGESTIVE BISCUITS

50g SUGAR

60g BUTTER

2 - 250g PKGS. LOW FAT CREAM CHEESE, SOFTENED

250g MASCARPONE CHEESE

15ml FRESH LEMON JUICE

60g WHIPPED CREAM

50g SUGAR

Prepare crust by placing the biscuits, sugar and butter in the 1.1L Processing Bowl. Pulse until fine crumbs form. Press into a springform pan and refrigerate.

Meanwhile, mix together the remaining ingredients in the 1.1L Processing Bowl until smooth. Pour into the crust and chill for at least 1 hour before serving. Serves 12.

CAL 357, FAT 29G, SAT FAT 18G, CHOL 80MG, SODIUM 236MG, CARBS 20G, PROTEIN 8G, FIBRE 0G, CALCIUM 64MG, POTASSIUM 100MG

ALMOND SOUR CREAM CHEESECAKE

250g LOW FAT CREAM CHEESE, SOFTENED

100g SUGAR

5ml ALMOND ESSENCE

2ml VANILLA ESSENCE

2 LARGE EGGS

230g SOUR CREAM

21cm PREPARED DIGESTIVE BISCUIT CRUST

35g SLICED ALMONDS, TOASTED

Preheat the oven to 160-170°C/Gas Mark 3. Position the Dough Blade in the 1.1L Processing Bowl and add the cream cheese, sugar, almond essence, vanilla essence, eggs and sour cream. Pulse until smooth. Pour the filling into the prepared crust and smooth the top.

Bake for 25 minutes or until set in the center. Remove from the oven and let cool. Top with the toasted almonds. Serves 10.

**CAL 311, FAT 16G, SAT FAT 6G, CHOL 67MG, SODIUM 270MG,
CARBS 35G, PROTEIN 7G, FIBRE 4G, CALCIUM 108MG, POTASSIUM 108MG**

anti-aging, skin, hair & eye health

immune boost

anti-inflammatory

immune boost

mental boost

anti-aging: skin, hair & eye health

detoxify & manage weight

digestion

energy boost

BERRY BERRY CRISP

FILLING:

**660g MIXED STRAWBERRIES, BLACKBERRIES
 AND RASPBERRIES**

100g SUGAR

30g MINUTE OR INSTANT TAPIOCA

5ml FRESH LIME JUICE

TOPPING:

40g WALNUTS, CHOPPED

60g BUTTER, CUT IN SMALL PIECES

60g UNBLEACHED, PLAIN FLOUR

65g SUGAR

1g BAKING POWDER

PINCH SALT

Preheat the oven to 190°C/Gas Mark 5 and lightly coat a 23 x 23cm baking pan with cooking spray. Set aside.

Place the mixed berries in a bowl and add the sugar, tapioca and lime juice. Toss to coat evenly. Spoon into the prepared pan.

Place the walnuts, butter, flour, sugar, baking powder and salt in the 1.1L Processing Bowl. Pulse until the walnuts are chopped and the mixture is crumbly. Scatter the topping over the fruit and bake for 35 to 40 minutes until bubbly. Serves 8 to 10.

**CAL 176, FAT 7G, SAT FAT 3G, CHOL 12MG, SODIUM 58MG,
CARBS 28G, PROTEIN 1G, FIBRE 2G, CALCIUM 15MG, POTASSIUM 110MG**

PUMPKIN PIE

1 MEDIUM SUGAR PUMPKIN, CUT IN HALF;
   STEM, SEEDS AND STRINGY PULP REMOVED
375ml CAN EVAPORATED MILK
140g DARK BROWN SUGAR
3g SALT
3 EGGS

6g GROUND CINNAMON
2g GROUND GINGER
PINCH GROUND NUTMEG
PINCH GROUND CLOVES
1g GROUND CARDAMOM
23cm PÁTE BRISÉE (SEE P. 183)

Preheat the oven to 180°C/Gas Mark 4.

Place the sugar pumpkin halves on a lined baking sheet and bake, cut-side down, for 1 to 1½ hours, until flesh is very soft. Remove from the oven and let cool. Scrape out the pumpkin flesh.

Place 240g of the pumpkin flesh in the 1.1L Processing Bowl and pulse until smooth. Spoon into a large bowl and add the remaining ingredients except the pie shell. Mix to combine and pour into the prepared pie crust. Bake for 1 hour until lightly browned and the middle is firm. Serves 8.

CAL 351, FAT 14G, SAT FAT 6G, CHOL 93MG, SODIUM 247MG,
CARBS 49G, PROTEIN 8G, FIBRE 2G, CALCIUM 181MG, POTASSIUM 279MG

immune boost

mental boost

anti-aging, skin,
hair & eye health

digestion

energy boost

immune boost

mental boost

anti-aging: skin, hair & eye health

digestion

energy boost

MANGO PEACH FROZEN YOGURT

80g FROZEN MANGO CHUNKS

115g FROZEN PEACHES

225g LOW FAT VANILLA YOGURT

Place the mango, peaches and yogurt in the 1.1L Processing Bowl. Pulse until smooth. Serve right away. Serves 4.

CAL 102, FAT 2G, SAT FAT 2G, CHOL 2MG, SODIUM 85MG, CARBS 5G, PROTEIN 12G, FIBRE 1G, CALCIUM 103MG, POTASSIUM 213MG

FRUIT N' CREAM ICE CREAM

330g FROZEN FRUIT (MIXED BERRIES, STRAWBERRIES, PEACHES ETC.)

125ml DOUBLE CREAM (OR USE MILK OR LOW FAT MILK)

25-50g SUGAR

5ml VANILLA ESSENCE

Place all ingredients in the 1.1L Processing Bowl. Pulse until smooth. Serves 6.

**CAL 161, FAT 11G, SAT FAT 7G, CHOL 41MG, SODIUM 12MG,
CARBS 15G, PROTEIN 0G, FIBRE 1G, CALCIUM 31MG, POTASSIUM 133MG**

anti-inflammatory

immune boost

mental boost

relaxation &
stress relief

anti-aging skin,
hair & eye health

digestion

energy boost

FRESH MANGO FOOL

2 MANGOS, PEELED AND SEEDED
125ml SUGAR SYRUP
60g WHIPPED CREAM

Place the mango flesh and sugar syrup in the 1.1L Processing Bowl and pulse until smooth. Spoon the mango mixture into a medium bowl and fold in the whipped cream. Serve right away in stemmed glasses. Serves 4.

CAL 182, FAT 11G, SAT FAT 7G, CHOL 21MG, SODIUM 14MG,
CARBS 29G, PROTEIN 2G, FIBRE 2G, CALCIUM 30MG, POTASSIUM 184MG

CANTALOUPE MINT GRANITA

1 RIPE CANTALOUPE, SEEDED, RIND REMOVED, AND CUT INTO CHUNKS

15ml FRESH LEMON JUICE

30ml WATER

40g RAW, UNFILTERED HONEY

2g FRESH MINT LEAVES

Place all of the ingredients in the 1.1L Processing Bowl and pulse until completely smooth. Pour into a non-reactive dish or ice cube trays and freeze for 3 to 4 hours, until completely solid.

Just before serving, place the frozen cubes in the 1.1L Processing Bowl and pulse again until smooth. Serve immediately. Serves 4.

CAL 79, FAT 0G, SAT FAT 0G, CHOL 0MG, SODIUM 85MG,
CARBS 22G, PROTEIN 2G, FIBRE 1G, CALCIUM 18MG, POTASSIUM 371MG

mental boost

anti-aging, skin, hair & eye health

detoxify & manage weight

energy boost

anti-inflammatory

immune boost

relaxation &
stress relief

anti-aging: skin,
hair & eye health

PINEAPPLE GINGER
COCONUT SORBET

1 SMALL RIPE PINEAPPLE, PEELED, CORED, ROUGHLY CUT

15ml FRESH LIME JUICE

125ml LIGHT COCONUT MILK

100g CASTOR SUGAR

2g FRESH GINGER, CHOPPED

Place the pineapple in the 1.1L Processing Bowl and pulse until smooth. Pour into a medium bowl. Place all of the remaining ingredients in the Bowl. Blend until completely smooth and add to the pineapple. Stir lightly to mix.

Pour the sorbet mixture into the freezer bowl or tub of your ice cream maker and proceed as directed. Makes about 950g.

CAL 114, FAT 1G, SAT FAT 1G, CHOL 0MG, SODIUM 4MG,
CARBS 28G, PROTEIN 1G, FIBRE 2G, CALCIUM 15MG, POTASSIUM 124MG

TART BLUEBERRY SORBET

750g FROZEN BLUEBERRIES
170g RAW, UNFILTERED HONEY
2g LEMON ZEST
15ml LEMON JUICE

Working in batches if needed, pulse the blueberries in the 1.1L Processing Bowl until smooth. Place the blueberries in a large mixing bowl and add the honey, zest and juice. Mix well and place in your ice cream maker. Proceed as directed. Makes about 950g.

CAL 86, FAT 0G, SAT FAT 0G, CHOL 0MG, SODIUM 1MG,
CARBS 28G, PROTEIN 0G, FIBRE 1G, CALCIUM 4MG, POTASSIUM 40MG

anti-inflammatory

immune boost

mental boost

relaxation &
stress relief

anti-aging: skin,
hair & eye health

detoxify &
manage weight

digestion

energy boost

anti-inflammatory

anti-aging; skin, hair & eye health

GREEN TEA GRANITA

750ml WATER
3 GREEN TEA BAGS
85g RAW, UNFILTERED HONEY
15ml FRESH LEMON JUICE
FRESH MINT FOR GARNISH

Bring the water to a boil in a saucepan. Add the green tea and honey. Let steep for 15 minutes. Remove tea bags. Let cool and add the lemon juice. Mix to combine. Pour into ice cube trays. Let freeze for at least 3 hours, or until solid.

Place the frozen tea ice cubes in the 1.1L Processing Bowl and pulse for 30 seconds. Garnish with mint leaves and serve immediately. Serves 4.

CAL 129, FAT 0G, SAT FAT 0G, CHOL 0MG, SODIUM 1MG,
CARBS 35G, PROTEIN 0G, FIBRE 0G, CALCIUM 3MG, POTASSIUM 22MG